Job Interview Questions Series

SELENIUM **TESTING TOOLS**

INTERVIEW QUESTIONS
YOU'LL MOST LIKELY BE ASKED: SECOND EDITION

303
Interview Questions

VIBRANT
PUBLISHERS

Selenium **Testing Tools**

Interview Questions
You'll Most Likely Be Asked: Second Edition

ISBN-10: 1-949395-10-3
ISBN-13: 978-1-949395-10-5

Library of Congress Control Number: 2011913369

Table of Contents

Dear Reader,

Thank you for purchasing **Selenium Testing Tools Interview Questions You'll Most Likely Be Asked: Second Edition.** We are committed to publishing books that are content-rich, concise and approachable enabling more readers to read and make the fullest use of them. We hope this book provides the most enriching learning experience as you prepare for your interview.

Should you have any questions or suggestions, feel free to email us at
reachus@vibrantpublishers.com

Thanks again for your purchase. Good luck with your interview!

– Vibrant Publishers Team

facebook.com/vibrantpublishers

Selenium **Testing Tools** Interview Questions

Review these typical interview questions and think about how you would answer them. Read the answers listed; you will find best possible answers along with strategies and suggestions.

This page is intentionally left blank

Chapter 1

Generic Selenium

1: Explain Selenium exception test.

Answer:

The Exception test is expected to throw all exceptions that the webpage is supposed to throw. A class that's written to throw an exception can handle the expected exception using the test annotation clause. Remember that the exception has to be a .class.

2: Explain the various frameworks supported by Selenium.

Answer:

Selenium supports three types of frameworks – Data Driven, Keyword Driven and Hybrid. The Data Driven framework uses an external file such as excel, xml, csv, database etc. to build test cases. The Keyword driven framework uses an external file to store the keywords such as commands or operations. In a Hybrid framework, the external file may have a combination of both keywords and data.

3: Explain the testing types that are supported by Selenium.

Answer:

You can do Functional, Regression and Load Testing using Selenium. Functional testing checks the functionality of the software application. Regression testing checks the functional and non-functional aspects of the software after the software undergoes a change to make sure that it still conforms to the client requirements. Load testing is done to check how much load the software can handle at its peak.

4: Explain the restrictions of Selenium.

Answer:

Selenium has the following restrictions:

a) You can only test applications that are web-based
b) You can't test Mobile applications
c) Selenium does not support testing of Barcode readers and Captcha
d) You need third party tools such as JUnit or TestNG to generate reports.
e) Being free, you won't get any vendor support
f) You need to be familiar with some programming language.

5: Explain Selenese Language.

Answer:

The Selenese language is used for writing Selenium IDE test scripts. It is used like a programming language for writing test scripts that run on Selenium.

6: Differentiate between driver quit and driver close.

Answer:

The driver close command closes the current browser window running the command. The driver quit command is used to close all browser windows opened by the program including the current one.

7: Differentiate verify and assert commands.

Answer:

Both Verify and Assert commands are used to check the result of a given condition, whether true/false. While the Verify command does not halt or pause the program irrespective of the status, the Assert command will continue execution only if the condition returns true. A verification failure doesn't stop the program execution in case of a Verify command. But while using the Assert Command, if the condition is false, the rest of the conditions are not skipped.

8: What is the difference between find Element() and find Elements()?

Answer:

While both the functions are used to fetch the web elements in a page, there's a subtle difference. The find Element() function is used to find the first element on the webpage at the given locator. Find Elements() will return all elements pointed by the locator.

9: Explain Windows based popups and how they are handled in Selenium.

Answer:

Using Selenium automation tool, you can only test web applications. It won't handle Windows popups.

10: What are some practical risks with Selenium?

Answer:

Here are some of the issues with Selenium:

a) Selenium is good only for web-based solutions
b) No support extended for Bitmap comparison
c) Third party tools have to be depended upon for all types of reporting requirements
d) Unlike the competing commercial tools, there's no vendor support
e) The absence of object source makes it a challenge to maintain the objects

11: Explain the benefits of Selenium.

Answer:

a) It supports Python, C#, Java, PHP, Perl
b) It supports Linux, Mac OS and Windows
c) It has authoritative procedures to locate the DOM, CSS and XPath elements
d) Highly regarded Google-supported developer community

12: Explain the four parameter you have to pass in Selenium.

Answer:

The four parameters that you have to pass when using Selenium are:

a) Host
b) Port Number
c) Browser
d) URL

13: Explain the Selenium testing tool.

Answer:

Selenium is an open-source tool primarily used for testing web applications on different browsers. It is used to automate the tests carried out on the web browser. Selenium is a pool of different tools that can run on Windows, Mac and Linux. It supports multiple programming languages and most of the popular browsers' latest version. Selenium tests can be developed using Visual Studio, Eclipse or other IDEs. It has no formal support since it is an open source tool. But there's an open source community for Selenium that offers complete support. It can work in sync with tools like JUnit and TestNG to manage test cases and to generate reports. It can also perform continuous testing with tools like Jenkins, Maven, & Docker.

14: How does Selenium differ from the rest of the browser automation tools?

Answer:

a) Selenium, being an open source tool comes with zero license cost whereas most of the other tools such as UFT, Test Complete etc are paid ones. Hence, Selenium is appealing due to the license or subscription fee incurred on commercial automation tools.

b) Selenium tools provide support for customization, assuring flexibility in terms of tool integration. For example, tools such as TestNG and JUnit for managing test cases and generating reports.

c) A custom-built framework offers ample control over the features that are built into Selenium. It allows the addition of new features to be built into the framework.

d) It is extensible to the extent that the source code can be modified for integrations. In the case of UFT and Test Complete, integration can be done only with the support team's help.

15: Explain the various tools available with Selenium.

Answer:

Selenium comes with a suite of tools, each catering to different testing needs.

Selenium IDE: The IDE or Integrated Development Environment is a plugin for Firefox browser which is mainly used to create and run test cases that are generated in the IDE by recording [use the Record button] the interactions/navigation of the expected user work flow with the browser. Upon recording of the test cases, they can be re-played multiple times. Further these test records can be exported to diverse programming languages such as Ruby, Java, Python, etc. This Plug-in is exclusively accessible for Firefox.

Selenium Grid: With the Grid, numerous test cases can be run simultaneously on different machines. The Hub-Node arrangement enables parallel execution. The Hub takes charge of the tests being executed on different browsers with diverse operating systems. The various node test scripts can be written using diverse programming languages.

Selenium WebDriver: Each browser has its own driver on which the application runs. However, Test Reports or Testing images cannot be generated.

16: How do I choose the right Selenium tool?

Answer:

Selenium is generally used to automate web-based Functional test cases and Regression test cases. The specific suite of Selenium tool to use should depend on your application to test as well as your testing purpose. Selenium IDE can be used for rapid testing of simple test cases as it does not require any programming or scripting knowledge. Use Selenium Grid if you have enormous test suites that must be executed on multiple environments. Use Selenium WebDriver to test AJAX-based applications, to generate personalized test results and to perform tests on the Html Unit browser. Use Selenium RC for cross-browser and cross-platform testing as well for data driven testing.

17: Explain Selenium IDE.

Answer:

This is an interface that records and plays any Selenium workflow action without the user having to know any programming or scripting language. The IDE only supports Firefox as an addon for the browser. Recording of the test case execution is carried out on Firefox. It supports test case execution on other browsers with the help of RC or WebDriver. The IDE is accountable for User Actions that are recorded as they are implemented. These recordings can be exported as reusable scripts to be executed later. Scripts are usually recorded in HTML but can be converted to other supported languages too. It also has a reporting module for test results.

18: Which language is supported by Selenium IDE?

Answer:

The default command in Selenium is written in HTML but other programming languages such as C#, Java, Perl, PHP, Python and Ruby are also supported.

19: What is Selenium 1.0?

Answer:

Selenium 1, also known as Selenium Remote control (RC), tool is used for test automation. This tool can run automated tests for any web application in any programming language. Currently Selenium has client drivers for PHP, Python, Ruby, .NET etc that makes running test cases easier. The benefit of using RC is that it allows the use of remote browsers and reduces the need to change every line of code with respect to the growing number of languages.

20: Explain Selenium 2.0.

Answer:

Selenium 2 is otherwise known as Selenium WebDriver which combines the elements of Selenium Ver 1 and Web driver. Selenium Ver 2.0 is a successor of Selenium Ver 1.0. It accepts a command as sent in Selenium or through API and then sends it to the browser. So, a browser-specific browser driver is used to send the results. Unlike in Selenium Ver 1.0 where a server was required to run the tests, Selenium web driver does not need a special server to execute tests. The web driver will initiate the browser directly and will control the test.

21: In what ways can you spot the elements on a web page with the help of Selenium?

Answer:

Locators help to find the elements on Selenium IDE. Locator is a critical factor while writing automation scripts to find the GUI elements on the IDE. There are 8 locators in Selenium IDE that help to locate various elements:

a) **ID**: Ids are unique and can spot an element instantly.
b) **Name**: Though names are not unique, it is easier to locate an element using the name.
c) **Identifier:** The ID attribute is searched first and then the name is searched with the Identifier.
d) **DOM**: The DOM locator locates the elements that match the JavaScript expression.
e) **XPath**: When the element can be located in an XML Pack, use the XPath locator.
f) **Link**: Use Link Text for locating the named links in the IDE.
g) **CSS**: The CSS Selectors help identify the element in the IDE.
h) **UI**: The page set UI elements help to map the element's DOM node and the page's XPath.

22: What is the use of Selenium Grid?

Answer:

Grid is part of Selenium suite which can run tests simultaneously on many machines. This ability to run tests simultaneously on multiple machines is useful in spreading the load of testing across several machines. Selenium grid is used primarily in cases when all the browsers used for testing cannot run on the same platform.

This page is intentionally left blank

Chapter 2

Selenium IDE

23: Explain how would you add a Selenium IDE break point.

Answer:

You can insert Selenium IDE break points with the "Toggle break-point" option from the IDE. Press the Keyboard option "B" and choose it. You can mention many Selenium IDE breakpoints using this method.

24: Explain how to debug tests with Selenium IDE.

Answer:

You can debug tests in Selenium using breakpoints. You must first insert break points at strategic places within the code. While running the testcase, the execution will pause at the breakpoint. A blue colour button will let you resume the next statement. You can execute all commands simultaneously by using the "Run" button instead of blue colour button.

25: Explain the Selenium IDE restrictions.

Answer:

The restrictions of Selenium IDE are:

a) No Exception-handling
b) Allows only HTML-based languages
c) Can't read External databases
d) Can't read from external text and excel files
e) Does not support conditional statements such as if-else or select statement

26: What are the two Selenium IDE view modes?

Answer:

You can view Selenium IDE as a popup window or on the sidebar.

27: When can you expect the IDE test to fail in Selenium?

Answer:

a) When Selenium IDE fails to find the element because the locator changed
b) When the expected element failed to be available on the webpage and the process times out
c) When Selenium IDE tries to access an element, which does not exist

28: What are JUnit Annotations?

Answer:

Annotations give additional instruction regarding the commands that use them. The following are the JUnit Annotations:

a) The **@Test** annotation specifies that the method that's annotated is a test method

b) The **@Before** annotation means that the method has to be annotated before each test method

c) The **@After** annotation means that the method has to be annotated after each test method

d) The **@Before Class** annotation means that the method has to be annotated once before any test method is executed

e) The **@After Class** annotation means that the method has to be annotated once after any test method is executed

f) The **@Ignore** annotation specifies that the specific method should be ignored

29: Which is the format to view your script source?

Answer:

Your source file will be shown in the XML format in Selenium when you use the source view in the IDE.

30: Explain how a start-point can be set.

Answer:

The Selenium IDE start-point is set in two different ways:

On the keyboard, press the "S" key and choose the command where you need to insert the start point. Another option is to opt for "Set/Clear Start point" after command's right-click.

31: Explain Selenium IDE's capabilities.

Answer:

a) Selenium IDE is as capable as the commercial tools Silk Test, Test Partner, QTP etc.

b) It's an add-on for Firefox.

c) Selenium IDE supports recording of clicking and other actions like typing for making testcases.

d) The tester can playback the testcases using Selenium IDE in Firefox browser

e) You can export the suites and testcases to Selenium RC.

f) Step by step testcase debugging is made possible

g) Lets you insert Breakpoints

h) Supports Page-abstraction

i) Feel free to use user-extensions and add-ons

32: How can you export the Selenium IDE tests to Selenium RC using different languages?

Answer:

Selenium IDE lets you export the test cases to .Net, Java, Perl, Python, PHP and Ruby.

To export the testcases, use the following command:

a) Open the Selenium IDE testcase

b) Choose "Export Test Case As" option from File menu

33: Explain the procedure to set Selenium IDE user extensions.

Answer:

a) First you need to open the user-extensions.js file using

b) Notepad or a similar editor. If it's not available, you need to create one
c) Commit this file (user-extensions.js) when required
d) Choose Selenium IDE, Options menu, Options
e) Set the path to your user-extensions.js file in the Selenium Core extensions field (such as "seleniumcorescriptsuser-extensions.js")
f) Click OK
g) IDE Restart will reflect the extensions

34: Explain the key Selenium IDE structures.

Answer:

a) You can generate and run testcases using the Record and Playback features
b) You won't need recording. Instead, type in the tests using element locators
c) There's a feature exclusively available for debugging
d) You can assert each page's title
e) Test suites and single-mode tests can be run
f) You can export the testcase into Java, Python, Ruby or C#

35: Explain the two view modes in Selenium IDE.

Answer:

Selenium IDE contains two modes of views –

a) Table view
b) Source view

Among these two views, the default one given by Selenium IDE is the table view where the test case is represented in a tabular format. In Table mode, we can create, insert and edit the Selenese commands one by one. After each test, the played steps turn into a different colour. Every single action of the user is categorized into a command, target or value. In Selenium, the table format is the most preferred as it is simple and precise.

The second mode of view which is the source view, is represented in the HTML format. In this format, each step is treated as a row which contains the command, target and value in different columns. It is very similar to an HTML document in which we can add any number of rows and columns to each Selenese command.

Table View

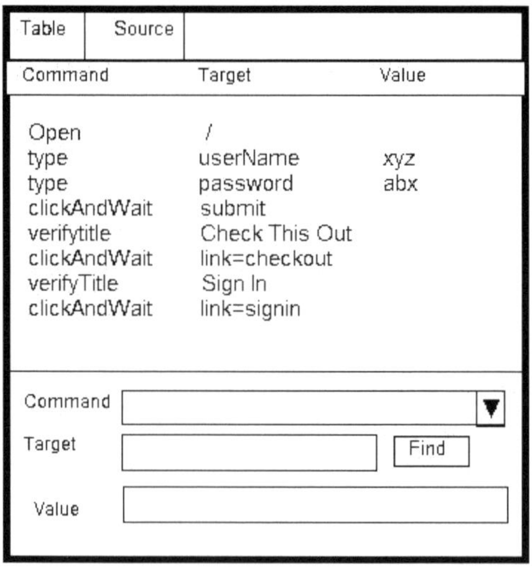

Source View

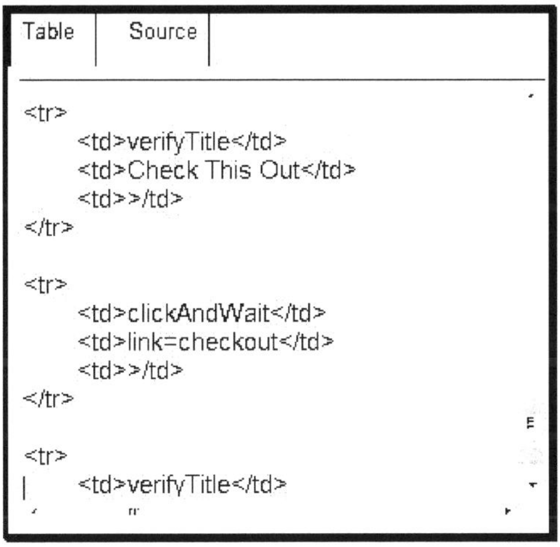

36: Can we regulate the test execution speed and pause in Selenium IDE?

Answer:

The toolbar in Selenium IDE puts forward a wide variety of options for recording and executing test cases. By using these options, we can determine and regulate the speed of recording and execution.

Playback Speed: This option helps the user to control the execution of each test case in the test suite. It helps to regulate the execution in fast, medium and slow modes according to the user's need.

Pause: This option helps to pause the test execution during runtime. It helps the user to test in a simpler and efficient way. If the pause button in the toolbar is clicked while the process is being executed, the entire execution is stopped.

37: I want to see the test results of Test Execution. How do I do that in Selenium IDE?

Answer:

The Log panel can be found at the bottom-most side of the Selenium IDE which shows the runtime messages during the test execution. Real time updates will be shown in Selenium IDE. Messages regarding error, information, and progress are displayed on this pane automatically during the execution of the test case. This method of displaying helps in debugging the test case more quickly.

Logs can be classified into four types:

a) **Debug**: This shows the technical errors in the current test step. The debug option can be activated from the filter on the right side.
b) **Info**: Information about the test step that is running currently.
c) **Warn**: Warning messages are shown when some errors occur.
d) **Error**: These messages are shown if the test fails in the execution.

38: How can I view command descriptions in Selenium IDE?

Answer:

A brief description of each command is displayed in the Reference pane. It provides the argument details with the description of the commands. In table view mode, the description of the current command is documented and displayed in the reference pane. The commands from the table view mode or the source view mode can be entered or modified in this pane. But for that, all parameters specified in the target and the value fields must match the parameter-list mentioned in the reference pane. The brief description helps the testers to understand the outcome of the test easily.

39: Can Selenium IDE be used to build test suite?

Answer:

Selenium IDE can be used to build test suite which is a collection of test cases. Each test case can be executed separately, or all put together as test suites. Like test cases, test suites are also created in HTML files. We could create test suites by selecting file>new test suite. Give a name to the newly created test suite and click OK. The test suite refers to the test cases as anchor elements. The anchors are present in a table of one-column and as many rows as in the test suite. The title of the test suite can also be seen in the table.

40: Explain the verification points in Selenium.

Answer:

Selenium has four tools - Selenium IDE, Selenium RC, Selenium Web driver and Selenium Grid. If Selenium IDE is being used, then Assert and Verify commands can be used as verification points. If we use Selenium web driver, then it doesn't have built-in verification points. A programming language as Java or Python or C# with control statements can be used as a verification point. There is no fixed number of points available. It depends upon the style of programming and the logic used.

41: How does verification and assertion differ in Selenium?

Answer:

The two types of checks, verification and assertion, are utilized to check if an input is available on the given webpage. There are differences between Assert option and Verify option in Selenium. If the assert command is not successfully executed, the test is aborted. When the execution is aborted, the steps beyond that line are skipped. So, if the assert condition is true, the test steps following the condition are executed but otherwise, the execution will be aborted, and the upcoming test steps will be skipped. When the verify command does not execute successfully, the test will be continuously executed and failure is reported. So, the test execution is not stopped even if the verify-condition is false.

42: How to add checkpoints to tests in Selenium IDE?

Answer:

Checkpoints compare the expected value of object to the objects' current values during a running session. During functional testing, click on the design option on the top of the Selenium IDE and select the checkpoints in the dropdown. It then displays the different types of checkpoints. Now by clicking on the desired checkpoint add them to the tests.

43: How to perform edit tests in Selenium IDE?

Answer:

In order to edit tests, the line which needs to be changed or edited is selected in Selenium IDE and then it is edited using command, value field. This type of editing or viewing is Table view. Another way is to see the source-code in which the source view is and modify the line required, be it command, parameter or comment.

44: Explain the command syntax in Selenium.

Answer:

The syntax of command used in Selenium has three parts, the first being the command name and other two the parameters. The parameters always depend on the type of command. If the command requires then both parameters are used else none of them is used. The parameters are mainly a locator, the target, or some kind of text pattern for entering text.

45: Out of the available Selenium commands, which commands are more frequently used?

Answer:

Pertaining to the application, one needs the relevant commands available from the tons of Selenium commands. Each command fulfils and serves a specific intent. One needs to identify why the application event or action is required and use the right command from the existing set of Selenium commands.

a) Use **Actions commands** to click a button, select an option from the dropdown box etc.

b) Use **Accessors commands** to appraise an application state and store the results in a variable. E.g. Store All Fields (Variable Name) – the IDs of all the input fields on the targeted page is stored in this variable and IDs of the same are returned when fetched for this variable.

c) Use **Assertions commands** to verify (e.g. at least one option is selected from the dropdown box) as well as to assert (e.g. ensure the right page is displayed on clicking a page link)

46: Explain the use of ID and name in HTML in Selenium IDE.

Answer:

For any test, one needs to uniquely identify the element one intends to find, select or test. The element or the elements that are to be tested are identified using their attributes or properties like ID, Name, X path and so on. Selenium IDE facilitates the use of HTML code for identifying elements on a web page. On a given web page, the ID and name text input elements are identified by the values to the attribute name and id.

Example:

```
<html>
   <head>
       <title> ID and Name Attribute </title>
   </head>
   <body>
<p>
          <p id="element id"> ID Attribute </p>
<a name = "element name"> Name Attribute </a>
       </p>
     </body>
</html>
```

47: Explain XPath and its usage in Selenium IDE.

Answer:

XPath (XML Path) is a locating element used for locating nodes in an XML document.

It is a method of locating elements within the content of web application.

Here's the syntax to create XPath:

XPath = //tag_name [@ attribute = 'val']

where;

//: Choose CurrentNode.tagname is the name of a particular node @: Select attribute.Attribute is the node's Attribute name and value is the attribute value

XPath is best used when we don't have the appropriate id or the element's name we wish to locate.

Use XPath to either locate an element in absolute state (not recommended though), or in a relative state to another element that does have an id or name attribute associated with it.

Absolute XPaths: It holds the location of all elements from its root to find out the element directly and as a result most likely to fail with even the slightest changes to the element's path.

Relative XPaths: You can locate your target element based on the relationship it holds with its parent element or for that matter any element that is in close proximity with your target element having an ID or name attribute associated to the element. This is less likely to change and can make your tests sturdy.

XPath axes are used to find dynamic elements or elements whose attributes change dynamically on clicking the refresh button or on performing any operations.

48: Explain Selenium CSS location strategy.

Answer:

This strategy envisages the web elements (one or more) by stating its attributes i.e. property and/or hierarchy of the target elements. This does increase its complexity of use, though. CSS locator is flexible and widely used. It gives a worthy balance between using structure-based and attribute-based locators. It can be used to find or select elements that have no ID, Name or Class. CSS can help to find out element substrings, especially the dynamically generated ones. You can even convert your XPath locators to CSS – preferred option for browser, more so for IE testing. It is of utmost significance to come up with the CSS string for the target element to be selected. This is largely based on one's experience as well as on capturing the right scenarios. It's advantageous to have good knowledge on the application you are testing, in terms of features most prone to usage, what could possible change and so on. You need to build/update your CSS strings so that it captures exactly what you intend from the web page.

49: Which one to choose among ID, name, XPath, CSS locator?

Answer:

Locators enable you to interact with a web page through its elements. While each locator does serve its purpose, each has its own pros and cons. It is best to select a locator that's cross-platform compatible, maintainable and reliable.

Locating an element on the web page by its ID is the easiest, most efficient and quick. However, the IDs need to be unique and fixed. In the absence of unique IDs, you will have to opt for other alternate locator options.

Locating an element on the web page using its Name is the best alternative when the IDs of the web element to be found are unknown or not available. Often the name is reused multiple times on a web page so ensure that the name is unique prior to using this locator option.

Locating an element on the web page by its XPATH renders precise locators. It is used for any and every XML and HTML (xHTML) document but this is not the preferred locator for cross-browser testing.

Locating an element on the web page by CSS is widely used and provides a good balance between structures and attributes. It enables to locate elements by their adjacent elements, but it does have a steep learning curve.

50: How to populate random numbers or dates in my test data?

Answer:

Random numbers or dates are always needed for the execution of test cases. At certain situations, we need to generate random variables to feed the test data. Even though Selenium IDE has no built-in command or function to generate random numbers, if we have a deep knowledge in Advanced Selenium IDE, it would be much easier. There are different methods to generate random numbers. One of the methods is using JavaScript which is the easiest. If we are using the store command, *'javascript{Math.floor(Math.random()*1000)}'* we could get the random numbers from 0 to 1000. As we have set the limit as 1000, we could get any number till 1000. We can set any limit. The store command will store the generated number into a variable so that we can use it anywhere in our test.

We can also use the excel sheets for storing key values for test data. There is a need for separate excel sheet for each test script and the test script name and the excel sheet used for it should be same.

51: How to store the result of an evaluation to use later in the test?

Answer:

To save the test results there is no built-in function or command. Instead, an add-on is available for the same. We can save and export the test cases and test suites using the plugin created by Samit Badle, named Test results (Selenium IDE). Firefox lets you install it in simple steps like other add-ons. After installation in file menu, we get two additional options as Export test case result and Export test suite result which will help us save the results in .html file to use the results in future.

52: How to print the stored evaluation result in Selenium to confirm its value?

Answer:

The simple command Echo allows you to print text to your test's output. This method helps to get the informational progress notes in the test which display on the console as the test is running. It is mainly used for debugging and for documentation in software testing tool. But it does not influence any kind of macro execution.

53: Explain how to handle JavaScript alert.

Answer:

JavaScript alerts are entirely different from the regular windows alerts because the alert appears as a blocking window and prevents the user from doing any action in the underlying window. If we are trying to do any kind of actions in the window beneath, an exception will come as: Unhandled Alert Exception: Modal dialog present.

There are mainly three different types of alerts - Simple alert, Confirmation alert and Prompt alert, present in the Selenium IDE. Selenium IDE will automatically handle the alerts by clicking OK in the same window which will prevent us from seeing the actual Alert. Selenium will not be capable of handling the alert if it appear in the page in the onload() function. It can be only handled when the page is completely loaded.

54: How to move my recorded XPath test to Selenium CSS locator?

Answer:

To locate XML nodes, we use Xpath language. The HTML files are another version of XML and we can use Xpath for locating HTML. The main advantage of using XPath is that we can access virtually every element even without name, id, class or attribute. But it comes with a lot of rules and is complicated when it comes to finding elements.CSS selectors, the string patterns, are used to spot elements based on a blend of HTML id, tag, class and attribute. Compared to other methods, CSS selector is complicated. But it is commonly used because it doesn't require any id or name to access an element. To convert test recording in Xpath to CSS locator use the following website: *http://cssify.appspot.com//*. If we are inserting Xpath in it, we will get the corresponding CSS locator.

55: I have scripted an element locator of my own. How to test the same?

Answer:

To test a locator, we have to first choose the locator and then try it. In the browser test editor, at the top side, we can edit the locator in the step editor option. If you test a newly created locator or an edited locator but failed to find any element, the only way is to repeat the step again. If it is actually a click step and something went wrong in between and do not have a return back option then we have to start testing from the beginning. Sometimes it is unable to find locator for the test cases. The Load Tester is a build in function in Selenium and hence, there are methods to assist this, like the Stack Overflow, support of the search engine etc.

56: Can the js extension be plugged into Selenium?

Answer:

Yes, it is possible to plug the js extension within the Selenium and use it smoothly. After creating the user extension, save it with the extension '.js'. you can save it any name convenient to you, but the only thing is it should be easily recognized. After that open Firefox and then Selenium IDE. On the opening window, click on tools and then click on Options. In the option Selenium core extensions, we can browse and select the .js file we have just saved and then click OK. The .js file will only be loaded if the Selenium IDE is restarted. To check and use the .js file, in an empty test we have to create a new command and see whether the Command dropdown list contains the .js file.

57: Explain the process for converting the tests for Selenium IDE from Selenese to some other language.

Answer:

There are many ways to convert the Selenium IDE tests from Selenese to other languages. As a default method, the tests in Selenium IDE is created in the HTML language or the Selenese language. To convert, at first, we have to install an Addon from seleniumhq.org. Then, open the Selenium IDE and from the menu bar opt for Options. From the Options select the Format option in which by default we cannot find any languages. In options check the 'Enable experimental feature' and click OK. That will add the languages and the user can select the desired one. Or else, in simple steps to convert to languages like Java, at first record the test as the usual method and then from the file menu select Export Test case as-Java/Junit4/Webdriver. Save the file with .java extensions which will convert the test into Webdriver.

58: Why am I unable to execute my converted Selenium IDE Tests in Java? Why am I unable to execute the options? Why is the Table tab of Selenium IDE disabled?

Answer:

The reason that you are not able to execute the tests is, your tests are not in the Selenese or the HTML language. Only in these two languages, Selenium IDE tests can be executed. While the tests are in other languages the execution options will be thus disabled. In the recording mode, the Red button will be enabled. If the test is in a different language it can be changed to HTML by selecting Options-Format-HTML. After converting to the HTML format, the execution will be enabled. While playing back the test should be in the table mode or else it will not work. Hence the table mode is disabled by default manner. There is no need to enable the table tab for executing the test written Selenese language.

59: How can I use Selenese only as my test script language and also run tests in other browsers?

Answer:

We can execute the tests written in Selenese language in many browsers. The reason behind this is the Selenium IDE is now available in both the Firefox and the Chrome. Different implementations are also available now. We could record the test suite in the Firefox and then it can be replayed in Chrome. Even though there are certain variations almost everything is similar and easily executed. The Selenium IDE is evolving and developing day by day. Thus, it is possible to execute Selenese tests in other browsers too.

60: How can we test a new command added in the middle of a program?

Answer:

To test only the new command, select that command and right click. Upon right click, the context menu is displayed. Select Play from the context menu.

61: Can you specify where the Selenium IDE tests should start test execution?

Answer:

To specify where Selenium IDE should start test execution, select the command line from the place you wish to begin your test execution, then select 'Start' from the Context menu.

62: What are the tools available (other than Selenium IDE) to test element locators?

Answer:

Other available tools for testing element locators are:

a) **XPath Checker**: a Firefox add-on that automatically generates Xpath for the web element. The add-on can be downloaded and installed like any other plugins.

b) **FireFinder**: an add-on for Firebug that can be used to test CSS as well as Xpath locators.

63: What are some of Selenium IDE's advanced upcoming features?

Answer:

The upcoming version of Selenium is version 4. It comes with the following features:

a) A web driver that's standardized for W3C

b) New Chrome Support with a new plug-in system and CLI runner based on node.js which will support web-based parallel execution and offer more insights

c) Improved Selenium Grid that's much easier to deploy. Once set up, the grid will become the hub and node as required

64: Explain how loops are used for flow-control in Selenium IDE.

Answer:

Loops are used to carry out a set of commands repeatedly. To use the loops with Selenium, install Flow Control addon to Selenium IDE (a flow control plug-in). This lets you make use of control flow statements such as goto, while-loop and gotoIf. The while-loop lets you carry out a set of statements until the while condition is satisfied.

65: Can screen coordinates be used with the click command, to click a particular portion of an element?

Answer:

Yes, the ClickAt command can be used to click on the specific part of the element. The ClickAt command syntax comprises of a locator for the element and the x, y co-ordinates. The default command used in Selenium IDE is Click for recording. To record the ClickAt commands, the recording mode needs to be changed in settings.

66: Explain how the drop-down option presence can be verified in Selenium.

Answer:

Assert_Select can be used to check the existence of drop-down selections in Selenium. Select is a class which provides different methods to select and deselect options on drop down object and multiple select objects.

67: In Selenium IDE, how to store information on a HTML table?

Answer:

The HTML Table command storeTable can be used to store information. It will store data of the targeted table cell. The data which is stored is from a specific row and column of the table. It can be written as below example:

storeTablecss=div > table 0.3

This will give the value of 1st row and 4th column.

68: Is it conceivable to have a high priority CSS-Locator in Selenium-IDE while recording and displaying the CSS and other locators?

Answer:

Selenium IDE's usual behaviour can be changed and higher priority to CSS locator can be given by creating a FILE of js type with the following information.

LocatorBuilders.myorder = ['css:name', 'css:id', 'id', 'link', 'name', 'xpath:attributes'];

This file can be saved with a Selenium IDE extension which is an option under Selenium.

69: How can we handle the dynamic alerts that appear on screen?

Answer:

In Selenium, two types of alert are focused upon. One is Windows-based alert pop up and the other is web-based alert pop up. A web-based alert can be handled in Selenium. Annoying popup alerts can be handled by checking for them and killing them before the actual action has to be taken. This can be tackled more efficiently by creating dynamic proxy objects and wrapping the WebElement with the proxy object.

70: Is right click allowed on a locator?

Answer:

Yes, right click is allowed on locator. This is made possible with the use of Actions class, leveraging the Action Builder.

71: How are screenshots of a page captured by means of Selenium IDE?

Answer:

Use these commands – capture Entire Page Screenshot And Wait or capture Entire Page Screenshot for taking the screenshot of the intended webpage while testing. Using a plug-in, you can also capture screenshots of all failed tests. The plug-in not only captures the screenshots but also generates a report.

72: Can the test execution be delayed after a particular command?

Answer:

The pause command is the wait command and useful in delaying the execution of the automated testing for a stipulated time. The time is expressed in milliseconds.

73: Explain page timeout and how it affects the Selenium script.

Answer:

The page Load Timeout command restricts the time that the script allots for a web page to be displayed. If the page loads within the allotted time, then the script continues to run. In case the page fails to load within the allotted time, then the script will be stopped by Timeout Exception.

74: Differentiate – type and type keys.

Answer:

The type command is used to specify a field value. The type keys command is used to simulate keystroke events associated with each key you type.

Chapter 3

Selenium RC (Selenium 1.0)

75: Explain the benefits of RC.

Answer:

The benefits of RC are:

a) Read or write data from and to excel files, text files, etc.
b) Can handle active objects and UI elements based on Ajax
c) Conditions and Loops improve efficiency and flexibility
d) Supports multiple Operating Systems and Programming languages
e) Selenium RC functions perfectly on all JavaScript enabled browsers

76: Explain a framework in general and the RC frameworks available.

Answer:

Framework is a group of classes and libraries. They help when testcases have to be automated. The following are the RC frameworks available:

a) NUnit
b) Junit
c) TestNG
d) Bromine
e) RSpec
f) unittest

77: Explain the technical restrictions of using Selenium RC.

Answer:

Selenium RC does not support the "same origin policy", which is a JavaScript restriction. Another restriction is that nothing external to the browser can be run.

78: Why do you need Selenium RC?

Answer:

Selenium RC helps to handle the programming requirements of test scripts such as conditional statements, loops, test result logs and reports, error and exception handling etc. which are not supported in Selenium IDE. Only HTML is supported by IDE. RC uses Python, Ruby, PHP and Perl languages to write test script programs.

79: How would you differentiate RC and Webdriver?

Answer:

The major difference between RC and Webdriver is in how they get the job done. The Webdriver leverages the browser's in-built capabilities while RC inserts JavaScript functions into the browsers when a webpage loads.

80: What is Selenium RC (also known as Selenium 1.0)?

Answer:

Selenium RC is a server-side program that is expected to remotely control a browser so that it can be invoked from anywhere.

81: What are the main components of Selenium RC?

Answer:

Selenium Remote Control is made up of two-components - Selenium RC Server and Selenium RC Client.

The RC Server communicates using the HTTP GET and/or POST requests. The server receives the client script, executes the same and returns the result to the server.

The RC client contains the programming language code [Java, Ruby, Python, Perl, PHP or .NET]. The client lets you create the script and communicate with the server.

82: Why do I need Selenium server?

Answer:

The Selenium server is desirable for Selenium RC test runs or for conducting WebDriver tests remotely on machines using the Selenium Grid. The Selenium server need not be run if only the

WebDriver API is used to run your tests and the browser and tests are run on identical machines. In such a case, WebDriver will automatically start the browser. Also, you may use the server:

a) when the Selenium Grid is used to allocate your tests across many virtual machines.
b) when connecting a remotely located machine using a specific browser version which is different from your native machine.
c) when not using the usual Java bindings like Python or Ruby; instead preferring the Html Unit Driver.

83: What is Selenium core?

Answer:

Selenium Core is considered the best testing-tool exclusively for web-based applications and it is based on Java. Tests in Selenium Core can be executed directly on the browsers such as IE, Firefox, Linux, and Macintosh. It comes with four components namely the IDE, remote control or RC, WebDriver and the Grid. You can run multiple tests simultaneously or separately on Selenium. The tests can be run on different browsers and they can be easily debugged.

84: Where is the executable for Selenium RC placed? How to install it?

Answer:

Selenium RC is a jar file in Java and doesn't have to be installed explicitly. You only need to download the compressed file and extract the server to the target directory. Prior to beginning any test, the server has to be started. Selenium comes with a library set in your choice of programming language. You can choose the language and then install the RC server and use the client-server driver for the specific language.

85: How to start the Selenium server after downloading both client and server libraries?

Answer:

Selenium RC server is a Java program. So, we first need to check if Java is installed in the computer. The Java version should be the same as the version which was installed and written on the command line. Then go to downloads on the Selenium page and download the same version of Selenium server standalone if it is not already present in the system. Now on the command prompt, type *java _jar <path>_port 4444* to the SELENIUM standalone file in the system, where 4444 is the port for the client to connect with Selenium RC.

86: Which other ports can be used if port 4444 is not free?

Answer:

Port 4444 is the port used for starting Selenium server by default. If an error message comes that says port 4444 is already in use/not free, then 5555 can be used instead. For example, *Java_jar<path>_port 5555*

87: How to start scripting in Selenium IDE?

Answer:

The first test script must be created in Selenium IDE by recording. Later, the script can be executed using the playback feature to see the functionality and success rate. It is then saved for future use. The format option can be used to change or convert the language of choice.

88: Can we start the Selenium server from program instead of the command line?

Answer:

If the Selenium server is not started manually through the command line prompt, then it can be started using a program code. The Java program code starts the Selenium server whenever it is called. There's another way to start the code, which is written inside the program and used when the port to be used is not specified.

```
SeleniumServer = new SeleniumServer ();
SeleniumServer.start();
.
.
.
SeleniumServer.stop();
```

89: How can I open the browser in Selenium?

Answer:

To open the browser, in the Java code, a default Selenium class is defined with four parameters. This class controls the browser and allows the usage of the browser in Selenium. The syntax to use this class is -

Selenium = new Default Selenium (host, port, browser, URL)

The host is where the Selenium Server is running, and the port used could be 4444 or 5555.The browser can be Firefox or Internet Explorer and the URL is of the website to open.

90: Do I need to install Java on my system even if am not using it to run my tests?

Answer:

Yes. Java was used for writing Selenium server and hence you need to install Java on your system.

91: What are the browsers compatible with Selenium?

Answer:

Selenium WebDriver and RC can support any available browsers like IE, Firefox, Chrome, Safari and Opera.

92: At the time of test execution, two browser windows are available one is the test application and another displays the commands being executed. Can you have a single window instead?

Answer:

This is possible by specifying 'singlewindow' while starting the Selenium server.

Example:

Java-jar < selenium server>. Jar-single window

93: Can I set a longer time for my test scripts so as to prevent time out?

Answer:

You can overcome the timeout issue by using the 'settimeout' method in your test scripts.

Another alternative would be to specify the time out while starting the Selenium server.

Java-jar< selenium server>.jar-timeout < time in seconds>

94: How to specify corporate proxy when your system is within a corporate network?

Answer:

At the time of launching the Selenium server you can specify the corporate proxy using

Java-jar <selenium_server>.jar – Dhttp.myproxyHost= <your_proxy_server> -Dhttp.myproxy.Port= <your_port>Dhttp.myproxyUser = <yourname>- Dhttp.myproxyPassword=<your_password>

95: Permission denied error is being displayed while switching domains like "yahoo.com" and "google.com". What is the reason behind this error?

Answer:

Every domain has its own origin policies. Usually, permission denied error is shown when violating the same-origin policies of domains or while switching protocols. This type of error can also appear when JavaScript is trying to locate UI objects which are not loaded. Hence, moving from "yahoo.com" to "google.com" is a restriction in JavaScript. To recover from this error, Selenium server should be started in the proxy injection mode using -

Java-jar<Selenium-server>.jar-proxyInjectionMode

Then the Selenium server will start working as a proxy server and switching domains will be possible during the test.

96: Using Selenium server, is it possible to execute the Selenese tests in other browsers? The test script should be Selenese and should be executed in browsers other than Firefox.

Answer:

Yes, it is possible to execute Selenese tests in another browser using Selenium Server. To execute Selenese tests in other browsers, we need to take care of certain parameters while opening and loading the Selenium server. The first one is the browser in which the test should be executed. Then, the test domain should be considered. After that, the paths should be considered, i.e. the path to the Selenese test suite and the path to the result of the test.

Java-jar<>.jar-
htmlsuite<browser><appURL><html_suite_path><test_result_path>

97: While a test is executed, can we log any number of options?

Answer:

Yes, we can log any number of options while a test is executed. Test Complete will generate a complete log of the actions that are performed during the execution of a test. It gives a clear idea of the summary of the test run, shows the passed and failed test cases and the reasons for it. It can be viewed in standard and tree views which provide a complete picture of the execution. During execution, we can see the log by selecting browser Side Log. For that, we need to start the Selenium server as *Java-jar<>.jar-browser Side Log*

98: Will Selenium RC work on UNIX/Mac?

Answer:

Yes, it is possible to use Selenium RC in UNIX or MAC as these operating systems can run Java programming language. On Linux,

MAC or Unix, open terminal window and change to remote control. Run *rc.sh* to open and start the remote control server. The remote control service will then be attached to the terminal and write its log to the standard output. The service can be stopped in between by pressing CTRL+C. The service can be run in the background also, if required.

99: Can we execute the test scripts in newly created experimental browsers? If yes, how?

Answer:

In Selenium RC, we can specify a path to a particular browser. This method is really helpful when we have different versions of the same browser, experimental browsers or a browser which is not supported by the Selenium RC. The browser setting can be done in the run mode with the option **custom* along with the path of the browser - to be used as **custom<path_to_the_browser>*.

100: After executing test cases, why don't I see the generated test report?

Answer:

Selenium does not have built-in report generation. However, it does support reports. For example, JUnit uses the ant plugin to generate test report or if you are testing with TestNG then TestNG generates reports.

101: Does Selenium have recovery scenarios similar to QTP?

Answer:

In Selenium, recovery scenarios are inherent to the programming language used for scripting. In case of Java, you can make use of

Exception handling. E.g. if you are trying to read data from a file which may be unavailable, then use the 'try catch' block to handle such exceptions. Use your code statements to continue test execution irrespective of missing file or other errors.

102: How do I iterate through my test script?

Answer: Iteration can be done by using loop statements for a given programming language. For example, to insert a set of different data to a text box, use the 'for' loop in Java as given below:

// Test data collection in an array

String[my]test data ={" tst1", "tst2", "tst3"};

//Iterate through each test data

for (String t :mytestData) {selenium.type("elementLocator", mytestData)};

103: How do I count the number of images on my page?

Answer:

Use the getEval() method which stands for 'get evaluator' to count the number of images on your page. Pass the following DOM statement to getEval() -

selenium.getEval("window.document.images.length;")

This will offer the total number of images on the page by counting the number of image links on it.

104: What are the existing choices while starting Selenium Server?

Answer:

To know the available options when you start Selenium server, use the "-h" option along with the Java -jar .jar command at the start of the server. Some of the options available are – browserTimeout, debug, jettyThreads, log, port, role, and sessionTimeout.

a) **BrowserTimeout** is the waiting time in seconds for a browser session to hang on while a WebDriver command is being executed.
b) **Debug** will enable the log
c) **jettyThreads** is the same as **jettyMaxThreads** where the maximum number of Jetty threads allowed is specified.
d) **Log** is used to specify the logfile name
e) **Port** is used to specify the server port number which by default is 4444
f) **Role** can be hub, node or standalone
g) **SessionTimeout** is the maximum time the server will wait for a response before it is killed.

105: Can you run your test-code using your own Firefox profile?

Answer:

In order to execute your test scripts on Firefox, you will have to pass the Firefox profile to Firefox driver and create an instance of Firefox. Then you must stipulate its file location. You can do this with the command *Java-jar.jar – myFirefoxProfileTemplate "your file location"* as you start Selenium server.

106: How is the Selenium server's log captured?

Answer:

To capture the server-side log, you need to restart your server as *Java-jar.jar –log selenium.log*. Selenium shall start adding the server-side notifications into the log.

107: Explain Heightened Privilege Browsers.

Answer:

Privilege Browsers are the browsers that are not limited by JavaScript's origin policy. As the name suggests, they enjoy higher privileges. For example, Internet Explorer and Firefox have higher security authorizations. When Selenium runs the applications under test, the browser will usually block the scripts but when launched in privilege mode, it will let the scripts run as a special case.

108: How to manage an application with many popup windows?

Answer:

To manage the popup windows, close them using Selenium commands and then come back to the main window. In the below example, on click of an image a popup window opens.

```
// click an image that pops up a new window
selenium.click("css=img");
// waitperiod for popup is set with anchor target "scs"
selenium.waitForPopUp("scs", getWaitPeriod());
//wait for scs seconds and then open the popup window
selenium.selectWindow("scs");
// Close the popup window and return to the main window
// When the argument is null, the Main window gains control
selenium.close(); //closes the popup window
selenium.selectWindow("null"); //control shifted to main window
```

109: When you execute a Firefox test, an error shows up that Firefox won't shut down when it is getting a profile ready. How to resolve this error?

Answer:

This error implies that Selenium is unable to start the Firefox browser since it is currently running on your system. So, you have to shut down all the Firefox browser instances currently open including the hidden Firefox profile that is not visible onscreen but is running in your system. The Firefox browser can be shutdown using the close() or quit() commands. Killing all Firefox processes will ensure your tests run smoothly.

110: Using Selenium RC, how can we execute the tests which contain AJAX operations?

Answer:

AJAX is a technique used to perform out-of-the-band HTTP requests from a webpage to a server and retrieve data to web page. AJAX stands for Asynchronous JavaScript and XML. Tests involving AJAX usually fail during operations and hence you may wait for the completion of AJAX calls. Running AJAX operations during the tests can be accomplished using the JavaScriptExecutor interface. When the jquery execution is finished, it returns jQuery.active = 0, which is used in Wait.Until process until the script returns true.

111: During the execution of a test, can we upload files, for example, Word file?

Answer:

If the file is in the same system or mapped network drive then, to upload the file, just type the path of the file to the file upload control.

If the file is to be transferred from a local to remote machine and then uploaded, then FileDirector should be set.

112: While running Selenium tests "permission denied error" is displayed. What can be the reason for this?

Answer:

The basic reason for the "permission denied error" in Selenium is the '*Same Origin Policy*' constraint in JavaScript. *Same Origin Policy* mandates that for a webpage's script to access data on another page, both the pages should have the same origin or port number, host name and URI scheme. For avoiding such kind of errors, it is better to use heightened privilege browsers.

113: Elements cannot be located using the "style" attribute with Internet Explorer. Why?

Answer:

While using the Internet Explorer, the "*style*" attribute may not work in certain situations. That's because the Internet Explorer, being not case-sensitive, will interpret the style parameters which are in upper case unlike other browsers that are case-sensitive. Hence, you can locate an element using *style* and lower case in any browser except Internet Explorer. This problem will only exist when you are locating elements used in multiple browsers. If you specify the locator to be used only in IE, this problem will be solved.

114: What are the technical drawbacks of Selenium RC?

Answer:

Selenium RC comes with a few limitations.

a) The architecture of Selenium RC is very complicated. Selenium

RC will function only when the browser and commands are aptly supported by each other.

b) JavaScript used by Selenium RC is Selenium core which makes the Selenium RC much slower when compared to others.
c) The commands in Selenium RC are confusing which makes it difficult for the testers to select the codes that are to be used.
d) It can only be operated in real and visible browsers and cannot support the headless HTMLUnit browsers.

115: Can testing code use objects outside the browser if required and how?

Answer:

The Robot class can be used for testing code using objects outside the browser. It interacts with events during browser automation. This class is a part of the AWT package of JAVA. This gives control over the input output devices attached. This class is not handled by Selenium web driver.

116: Can Selenium be used for browsers on mobile devices?

Answer:

Selenium cannot be used for testing mobile browsers but there are frameworks based on Selenium which can be used for testing mobile applications. There are basically two types of frameworks. The first one is Selendroid and as the name says, it is for the Android operating system. The other one is Appium which can run on both Android and IOS platforms. The test script can be written in languages that are compatible with Selenium.

117: What are the advantages of Selenium RC compared to other tools?

Answer:

What makes Selenium the most advantageous over other tools is that Selenium runs on multiple platforms and browsers. This helps because the code can be written in any language without worrying about the platform on which it will be run. The languages which can be integrated with Selenium are Java, .NET, Ruby, Perl, Python, PHP and JavaScript. Selenium RC or Selenium Remote control server helps in creating test structures which are spread in different locations.

118: What are the disadvantages of using Selenium RC?

Answer:

A few disadvantages of using Selenium are as follows:

a) Selenium supports web-based application but doesn't support desktop applications.
b) The test automation tool doesn't have support for Image testing.
c) Another tool needs to be integrated with Selenium if any kind of test management feature is required.
d) Report generation facility is not available. External framework of Junit or TestNG used for testing is required to produce test reports.

119: How can we run two tests on diverse browsers on the same operating system with Selenium RC?

Answer:

Selenium Grid is designed to run tests on two different browsers.

This is made possible with a framework like TestNG which will allow the use of two different browsers. In TestNG, the tests are executed parallelly which is how it allows two diverse tests to be run using different browsers. Parallel testing involves multiple executions which will ultimately have some level of dependency.

Chapter **4**

Selenium Grid

120: When is the Selenium Grid more advantageous?

Answer:

Selenium Grid is more advantageous when the test cases have to run faster or parallelly on different operating systems.

121: Can you record the Selenium Grid test cases from other machines? Explain how?

Answer:

Selenium Grid does not allow recording test cases.

122: Explain the working of Selenium Grid.

Answer:

The grid will send the tests first to the hub. From the hub, the tests are redirected to the Webdriver which launches the browser and runs the test. The grid is capable of running tests in parallel within the test suite.

123: Which component in Selenium Grid routes the requests in Selenese from the Test?

Answer:

The hub is responsible to route the test requests in Selenese.

124: How many maximum browsers can parallel-run on a Selenium node?

Answer:

At the most, five browsers can run in parallel on a Selenium node.

125: What is the default number for hub port assigned?

Answer:

The default port number used by the hub is 4444.

126: Can you create test cases using test design in Selenium Grid?

Answer:

No, you cannot design test cases using the Selenium Grid.

127: What is the default Selenium Grid timeout?

Answer:

The default timeout set in Selenium Grid is 300 seconds.

128: Can Selenium RC and/or Selenium Webdriver test cases be executed in parallel using Selenium Grid?

Answer:

Yes, Selenium Grid allows to execute Selenium RC and Selenium Web driver Test Cases parallelly.

129: Can Selenium IDE Test cases be executed using Selenium Grid?

Answer:

No, Selenium IDE Test Cases cannot be executed using Selenium Grid.

130: Explain the two major Selenium Grid elements.

Answer:

The two major Selenium Grid elements are the Hub and the nodes.

131: How many hubs are available in Selenium Grid?

Answer:

The hub is single and controls the network in Selenium Grid.

132: How many nodes are available in Selenium Grid?

Answer:

The Selenium Grid can contain at least one node. There's no maximum limit for the number of nodes.

133: How to specify the browser and OS information in Selenium Grid?

Answer:

Desired Capabilities is used to set the browser type and the OS of our Node.

For example:

DesiredCapabilities mycapabilities = DesiredCapabilities.chrome();

mycapabilities.setBrowserName("chrome");

mycapabilities.setPlatform(Platform.WINDOWS);

134: How to reduce the test execution time of Selenium tests, when the test is executed using various machines and browsers?

Answer:

By using the method of parallel testing, we can run our tests in multiple browsers and multiple machines at a time. Parallel testing or testing different units or modules concurrently helps to reduce the time of execution for each test to a large extent and makes the entire testing process much faster. Moreover, multiple tests can be executed concurrently which further speeds up the completion of the testing process.

135: Explain the working of Selenium Grid.

Answer:

Selenium Grid permits to execute and run tests on different machines and different browsers at the same time concurrently. Distributed test execution method is supported by Selenium Grid. Suppose the machine in which our code is present is taken as the hub, then all other machines with different configurations must be registered as nodes to the hub. When the instruction to execute the code is given to hub, it checks the nodes connected, selects the one that has a similar configuration and sends the command to execute. The code will be present and execution happens in the hub, but the browser in the node machine performs each step of the code in the node machine.

136: Picturize the functionality of Selenium Grid.

Answer:

The Selenium grid consists of a hub and many nodes attached to the hub. The hub receives a request for testing an application on a particular platform and browser combination. The hub will identify the node that has this platform/browser combination among the attached ones and will wait to run the test. The node that receives the test request will perform the test. The following diagram represents the functionality of Selenium grid.

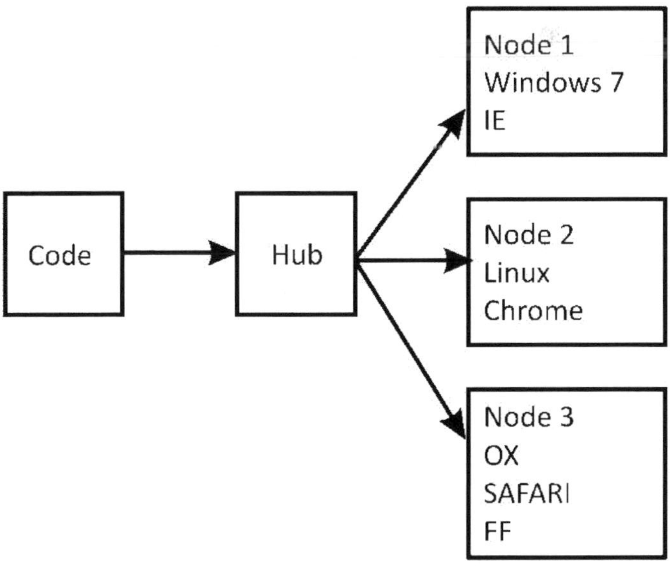

137: How do you configure Selenium Grid Hub?

Answer:

Selenium Grid Hub can be installed in the following steps:

a) Download Selenium IDE jar version you want
b) Make sure Java is installed on your system
c) Make sure that Java and the JAR files are in the same folder
d) At command prompt run the Java command to run the application packed in the downloaded jar file. In the same command, the role of the machine should be set to hub with the *-role hub* flag.

138: How do you configure Selenium Grid Node?

Answer:

Selenium Grid Node can be installed in the following steps:

a) Download Selenium IDE jar version you want
b) Make sure Java is installed on your system
c) Make sure that Java and the JAR files are in the same folder
d) At the command prompt, the web driver path should be set to that of the browser's driver followed by running the jar file. Along with this, the role should be set to node and the node should be registered under the hub's IP and port.

139: How can you start the Selenium Grid Slave Server?

Answer:

Selenium grid has a Hub-node architecture where one Hub acts as the master and the nodes act as slaves. The Selenium server JAR file needs to be downloaded from the Selenium website. Once the file is saved in the download directory, navigate to the file and execute the *ant* command to launch the remotely controlled server which will listen to the port number 555. This remotely controlled server will be listed under remote control servers available as slaves for Selenium grid servers.

140: Can you start the Selenium grid's slave from another port than the typical 5555?

Answer:

Yes, command DPORT can be used along with the port number for initiating the Selenium grid slave on the specific port. For example, ant -DPORT = 2222 *launch-remote-control* will launch the Selenium grid slave in 2222 port.

141: How can you start the Selenium grid slaves on different systems so that the hub can be controlled by the local host?

Answer:

The RC slave can be invoked by the command *ant -myPort= -myHost = -myHubURL= launch-remote-control* to run a separate process for the test suite. Java framework uses *ant* script to invoke this where it would first identify the machine which is chosen as the hub and the port on which the hub service will get started. The *myHost* indicates the host on which the RC slave is currently running while my Hub URL gives the machine URL which is identified as a hub.

142: Can an environment be specified when you start the grid slave?

Answer:

Yes, the environment can be specified when you start Selenium grid slave on a system. As Selenium grid is used to distribute the test in different environments and platforms, this can be done using the *-DEnvironment* command when the Selenium grid slave is started.

143: How do you use Selenium test configuration specific to a machine?

Answer:

Machine-specific Selenium test configuration can be specified using the following commands: For example, consider two machines, one having Windows 7 and Windows 10, in use. This creates two hubs and two nodes where the nodes are to be registered with the same hub. So, Windows 7 will have the hub started with the jar file running as an application and set as the hub. Then, the first node is registered on the node machine with WebDriver and the hub set. Register the second node on Windows10. Open the console on a machine that runs Windows-7 if you want to check whether all nodes are in the hub.

144: How can you map a name like 'Safari on Mac' to Safari Browser?

Answer:

Name-mapping in Selenium grid can be done using the "grid_configuration.yml" file that defines the configuration of all the browsers. Once you add this file to your project, the mapping can be done.

145: How will the Selenium grid hub contact the RC slave?

Answer:

The hub polls every RC slave at pre-set periods to ensure their availability for testing. In case of unavailability of any RC slaves,

Selenium hub disconnects from that RC slave and is accessible to all the RC slaves that are test-ready.

"*remoteControlPollingIntervalInSeconds*" is the deciding configuration parameter defined in the yml file named "grid_configuration" to effect the same.

146: The RC slave can, at times, become unresponsive while the Selenium grid hub waits for the its response. How does the hub recognise to leave the waiting RC slave afterwards a while?

Answer:

You can set a waiting time for Selenium grid hub on an RC slave. When the RC slave fails to respond within this stipulated timeframe, then the hub must disconnect the execution of the test on the slave by implementing the "*sessionMaxIdleTimeInSeconds*" configuration parameter defined in "grid_configuration.yml" file.

147: What happens if the hub becomes unavailable when the Selenium RC slaves are running?

Answer:

There is a "heartbeat" mechanism that sends a signal between RC slave and hub. The "*hubPollerIntervalInSeconds*" parameter is used by the RC slave for keeping track of all grid hubs that are running. You can define this parameter when you start the hub with "*ant -DhubPollerIntervalInSeconds= launch-hub*". It is used to specify the waiting time. When the hub fails to respond in a specified time, then the RC slave will deregister itself from the hub.

148: Can you use the Selenium grid for performance testing?

Answer:

The performance test is typically carried out on a replicated HTTP request-response setup. Otherwise, it involves huge investment in terms of software and hardware in case the performance test has to be run on an actual Selenium grid.

149: While working with Selenium Grid, can we use additional logs?

Answer:

Yes, we can use additional logs when working with the Selenium Grid. The logs of Selenium grid hub can be seen in the log folder in hub.log and the logs for Remote control machines can be found in the folder of "log/rc-*.log"

150: How can you run the RC Slave in single-window mode?

Answer:

The Java property "SeleniumArgs", can be used when starting the remotely controlled machines. By setting the *ant* command's-*DseleniumArgs*parameter to '-singleWindow -debug' *launch-remote-control*" option, we could run the RC slave machine in a single window.

151: A similar RC slave is displayed multiple times in the hub console. What may be the reasons for these duplicate entries?

Answer:

This happens when we try to kill the RC slave in an improper method. If the RC slave connection is not closed properly, while closing, these kinds of duplicate entries can be found in the hub.

These kinds of duplicate entries can be avoided by closing the remote machines in explicitly and then restarting the hub. After doing this the remote machines or the slaves will get automatically registered to the hub.

152: During the initialization of Selenium grid, is it possible to set the corporate proxy?

Answer:

We can set the corporate proxy while beginning the Selenium hub and/or remote machines by setting the changes in proxyHost and proxyPort files. The *ant* command is used to launch the hub and remote control.

153: While using languages such as .Net, Ruby, or Java, how can Selenium drivers be used?

Answer:

Selenium drivers are used to work with the testing script languages. These are basically libraries which contain the Selenium API commands which can be used as methods or functions. Web applications are usually tested using the test automation tool Selenium for which there is no testing framework. Some specific testing frameworks can support Selenium. For instance, for Java, we can use JUnit and TestNG. For Ruby, we can use Rspec. Likewise, for each language, there is a need for specific frameworks to support Selenium.

154: What do you know of the test reports while using Selenium grid to execute a test?

Answer:

Extent Report is one of the best tools that go with Selenium Grid. It is a simple open source tool to use and provides a dashboard for the entire test runs and even supports both TestNG and JUnit. However, it comes with certain prerequisites. You will have to ensure that the following are installed on your system; Java, Maven, Selenium TestNG and Extent Report Jars. With Extent report, you can create Pie charts and dynamic logs, generate step by step Test Case Summary, attach screenshots with errors to the report and even filter reports based on status.

Chapter **5**

Web Driver (Selenium 2.0)

155: Explain the limitations if any while inoculating competences in WebDriver to run tests on browser that is not reinforced by WebDriver.

Answer:

The major restriction of injecting capabilities lay in the fact that the command 'fundElement' will not function as desired as the webdriver uses Selenium's Core to force the capability injection effect. This is restricted by JavaScript's security features.

156: Explain the various exceptions in Selenium WebDriver.

Answer:

Selenium Exceptions are much like those in programming languages. Here are some of the most common ones used in Selenium:

a) **NoSuchElementException** - when an element with specified attributes is not there on the webpage

b) **TimeoutException** - when the command times out and does not complete execution within a stipulated timeframe
c) **StaleElementException** - when an element does not exist anymore in the DOM
d) **ElementNotVisibleException** - when an element is invisible on the webpage though present in the DOM

157: Explain the variety of WAIT statements in Selenium WebDriver.

Answer:

Selenium has two types of Waits – Implicit and Explicit Wait.

When you ask the Webdriver to wait for a while by specifying in the DOM, it is implicit wait. Through the Webdriver's instance, the implicit wait definition will be available. The value is usually zero by default and once a value is specified, it will periodically poll the DOM based on the driver implementation. In explicit wait, the wait continues until an event such as elementToBeSelected, presenceOfElementLocated or elementToBeClickable occurs.

158: Which API is essential for Selenium Webdriver Database Testing?

Answer:

The JDBC or Java Database Connectivity API lets you run SQL statements for Database testing while using Selenium Webdriver.

159: Explain the Selenium WebDriver listeners.

Answer:

There are basically two major Webdriver listeners – Webdriver and TestNG listeners. The Webdriver listeners will "listen" to the Selenium script events and act accordingly. You can thus customize TestNG logs and reports.

160: Explain the buzzword Selenium ver 2.0.

Answer:

Selenium ver 2.0 means Selenium ver 1 with additional features and benefits. What stands out with Selenium ver 2.0 is the new feature of Integration with Webdriver API. Selenium ver 1 works with any browser if it has a JavaScript engine, however, Selenium ver 2.0 would need a driver for that particular browser.

161: Why do you need to combine two tools as Selenium ver 2.0?

Answer:

Selenium ver 1 and the WebDriver are merged to create an improved version -Selenium ver 2.0, thus reducing the limitations of the RC server and overcoming the IDE shortcomings (only support for Firefox browser). The WebDriver has a modest and small programming interface that even addresses some of the limits of Selenium-RC API. It's a solid OO API in comparison with Selenium ver 1.0. It runs the browser more credibly and rises above Selenium ver 1.x's limits that affected the test reporting functionally like file uploading or downloading, dialogues barrier and pop-ups.

162: Will everyone be using Selenium ver 2.0?

Answer:

Not really. Depending on the driver support available for your client Selenium ver 2.0 can be used or else you might use Selenium ver 1.

163: How can you specify Selenium ver 2.0 browser configurations?

Answer:

There are only three popular browsers which are widely used - Google Chrome, Mozilla Firefox and Internet Explorer. However, Selenium supports other browsers too. To execute your script on different browsers you would need to mention the driver of each of the browsers you want to use.

164: Differentiate between Selenium ver 2.0 and Selenium ver 1.0 configuration.

Answer:

Selenium ver 1.0 is also known as Selenium RC and Selenium ver 2.0 is known as Selenium Webdriver. The major differences are as below:

a) In Selenium ver 1.0 a remote server is started before execution.

b) Selenium ver 1.0 supports some browsers like IE, Firefox, Chrome but Selenium ver 2.0 supports all browsers.

c) The core of Selenium ver 1.0 is JavaScript based. Every time, Selenium core is called to control and execute the browser while in case of Selenium ver 2.0 there is a direct interaction.

d) Selenium ver 1.0 has a built-in test result generator which gives an HTML file as the result whereas Selenium ver 2.0 has no built-in result file generator.

165: Give a coding example for starting Selenium ver 2.0 for testing.

Answer:

The coding example is as below

WebDriver myWbDrvr = new FirefoxDriver(); //this will launch a default firefox profile

myWbDrvr.get("www.facebook.com"); // launches a new browser session with opening the URL mentioned.

myWbDrvr.findelement(By. cssSelector("#gb_1 >span.gbts")).click(); //elements to be located in webdriver using css selector engine

166: In Selenium Webdriver, which one has the fastest implementation?

Answer:

The HTML unitdriver has the fastest implementation in Selenium. It won't run the tests on the browser which makes it faster compared to opening a browser before executing tests.

167: What are the different types of element locators present in Selenium ver 2.0?

Answer:

The locator normally used is Locating the element by ID and locating the element by class name are used when the software webpage has an element with an ID or a class name. In case, both are not present then Locating the Element by TAG Name can be used. The syntax used is as below:

find Element(By.tagName("select"));

The locating element by name is another useful locator. The syntax used is as below:

find Element(By.name("name"));

168: How would you submit a Selenium form?

Answer:

Selenium Webdriver uses a method name to submit any form. This method works in a similar way as clicking on a submit button. The code can be written as below:

WebElementmyWebElement = myWebDriver.findElement(By.id("ID"));

myWebElement.submit();

169: How would you stimulate the keyboard keys by pressing with the help of Selenium ver 2.0?

Answer:

While the test automation is done, we will have to press the arrow keys, tab, enter, alt, control key, function keys and non-text keys. We will be able to stimulate these keys during the execution in Selenium. We can use Keys enum, an option given by Selenium for the keys that we need to use.

Keys.Enter or *Keys.Return* will help us to sendKeys method to the textbox for clicking Enter for a textbox.

WebElementmytextbox =

mywebdriver.findElement(By.id("idOfElement"));

mytextbox.sendKeys(Keys.ENTER);

Another method is by using the following:

WebElementmytextbox =

mywebdriver.findElement(By.id("idOfElement"));

mytextbox.sendKeys(Keys.RETURN);

Likewise, we can write various Keys enums and send to the

sendkeys methods.

170: Explain how to clear the content of the textbox with the help of Selenium ver 2.0.

Answer:

To clear the text from a text box, use the method 'clear()'. It is a simple method to clear any text box. The following command can be entered to the test to clear the content inside the text box:

clearTheTextBoxField();

By executing such a command, with the help of CSS Path, it finds the location of the Text box field and clears the text inside the text box.

171: Using Selenium ver 2.0, how do you choose a value in drop down list?

Answer:

For working with the dropdown list, it is important to consider two things. At first, we need to import the package i.e.

org.openqa.selenium.support.ui.Select

The next step is to initialize the dropdown box like an instance, Selection object. This can be done by using three methods

selectByVisibleText

selectByIndex

selectByValue

By calling these methods with required data, we can create and control the drop-down list.

172: While working with Selenium ver 2.0 there may be popup windows displayed. Explain the options to deal with it.

Answer:

The users are offered different ways to handle the pop-ups. It can be handled using the Alert interface.

Along with Alert interface, we could use mainly four different methods. They are:

a) **Void sendKeys**() - Into an alert box specific string patterns are entered using the sendkeys().
b) **String getText()** - The text in the alert box is returned using this method.
c) **Void accept()** - When the popup window is displayed, automatically ok button is clicked and accepted.
d) **Void dismiss()** - When the pop-up window appears, automatically the cancel button is clicked and the window is closed.

173: With the help of Selenium ver 2.0, how to handle frames?

Answer:

An iframe is an HTML document which is incorporated inside an HTML document. In HTML, it is defined by the tagline <iframe></iframe> and using this allows us to identify the iframes. To switch iframes in between,switchTo().frame command is used. It is possible to use this in three ways -

switchTo.frame(int myFrameNumber)

switchTo.frame(string myFrameNameOrId)

switchTo.frame(WebElementmyFrameElement)

When passing these requests, the driver will switch to the mentioned frame.

174: Is navigating forward and backward in a Selenium ver 2.0 browser possible?

Answer:

Yes. The Navigate interface is used to navigate backwards and forward on a page. The Navigate interface methods contain - back, forward, refresh;

driverback.navigate().back()

driverforth.navigate().forward()

175: Which is the fastest WebDriver browser implementation order?

Answer:

The HTMLUnit driver implementation would be the fastest as it would not involve any interaction with the browser. Subsequently, would be the Firefox browser and next Internet Explorer.

176: Can you use Selenium ver 2.0 with Selenium RC API?

Answer:

You can use Selenium ver 1 RC API with Selenium 2. However, all the RC API methods are not supported with Selenium ver 2.0 and even the performance could be sluggish when Selenium ver 1.0 is simulated within Selenium ver 2.0.

177: Explain with an example – using Selenium ver 1 in Selenium 2.

Answer:

For this, you will need an instance of the Webdriver and use Selenium methods:

```
// Create a new instance of web driver
  WebDriver myWebDriver = new FirefoxDriver();
// Application URL
  String mySampleAppUrl = "https://www.google.com&#0014;;
// Get a new instance of Selenium
Selenium mySelenium = new WebDriverBackedSelenium(myWebDriver,
mysampleappUrl);
// Tests using new selenium instance
myselenium.open(mysampleappURL);
myselenium.type("name=SF", "testDatasample");
myselenium.click("name=mybtnG");
// Get back my instance of Web Driver
WebDriver mydriverInstance = ((WebDriverBackedSelenium)
myselenium).getUnderlyingWebDriver();
```

178: Selenium ver 1.0 had many supporting browsers whereas Selenium ver 2.0 only has a few. How do I use a particular browser with Selenium ver 2.0?

Answer:

Use the Capabilities class that permits new means to the Webdriver. Use this class to set your testing browser to say 'Safari'

Example:

```
//create an instance myCapabilities
SettingCapabilitiesmycapabilities = new DesiredCapabilities()
//Set my browser name
mycapabilities.setBrowserName("My Browser");
//My Browser execution capabilities
```

CommandExecutormyexecutor = new SeleneseCommandExecutor ("https:localhost:5555/", "https://www.google.com/&#2214". mycapabilities);

//Driver instance to the Capabilities you want

WebDriver mywebdriver = new RemoteWebDriver(myexecutor, mycapabilities);

179: Are there any restrictions when augmenting the Webdriver abilities while performing browser-based tests?

Answer:

The main limitation is in the usage of *find element* command which has limited capabilities and may fail to keep up to the expectations.

180: Can the user agent be changed in Firefox browser as the tests to be performed need to check the setting of user agent?

Answer:

Yes, it can be done with the *'about config'* command on the address bar of Firefox browser. Warning will be issued, as the settings changed would hinder the performance. On the filter box of *'about config'*, type *'user agent'* and check for *"general-useragent-override"* preference. If it is not present, right click on the config page, choose *new* and then, *string*. Now, name the preference and enter the value of desired user agent as its value.

181: Do different employments of the Webdriver have different XPath implementations?

Answer:

Yes, XPath can be absolute or relative. The absolute Xpath starts with the root element. For example, as html/head, whereas for relative

Xpaths it starts with the "//" symbol.

182: What can be done if the application is using AJAX largely, due to which the tests are getting timed out when Selenium 2.0 is in use?

Answer:

An implicit *wait* instruction can be given to the Webdriver till the element is available, when it is not available instantly. The default setting is 0 and it remains, as long as the Webdriver object is present.

183: Can anything else be used instead of implicit wait when wait is required for elements?

Answer:

Explicit wait can be used to wait for the availability of specific elements before resuming the test execution. "*WebDriverWait*" and "*ExpectedCondition*" can be used to achieve this as follows:

```
WebDriver myDriver = new FirefoxDriver();
WebElementmyDynamicElement = (new WebDriverWait(myDriver,
30)).until(new ExpectedCondition<MyWebElement>(){
@Override
   public MyWebElementapply(WebDriver myD) {
      return myD.findElement(By.id("myDynamicElement"));
   }});
```

This will wait for 30 seconds and then show *ElementNotFound* exception.

184: Explain what and when to use Remote WebDriver.

Answer:

There are different implementation classes for the interface of the Webdriver. Remote WebDriver is one among such implementation classes. In a remote machine, the user can test the scripts through the server of Remote Webdriver. Mainly there are two sections for the Remote Webdriver. They are client and server. The server of the Remote Webdriver tries to collect different requests from the client of the Remote Webdriver. When the requests are received, the server will send them to browser drivers of Firefox, Internet Explorer, Chrome etc as per the request. If the test is executed locally, then the client libraries of WebDriver communicate with the browser drivers directly. But when the test execution is done remotely, then the clients of Webdriver, at first, communicate with server of Remote Webdriver and then, it will communicate to the requested browser driver.

185: Which languages are supported by WebDriver?

Answer:

The programming language used in the Selenium is through the drivers. The languages include

a) C#
b) Haskell
c) Java
d) JavaScript
e) Objective C
f) Perl
g) PHP
h) Python

i) R

j) Ruby

186: Using Selenium WebDriver, explain the method to handle JavaScript alert.

Answer:

The Web-based alert or the JavaScript alert can be handled using the Alert interface. This interface provides certain methods to work with these popups. During the test execution, the control will be on the browser, and not on the alert popup. To control the alert popup, we need to use the command *"driver.switchTo().alert();"*. When we change the control to the alert window, we can use the methods of alert interface. By using these methods, we can accept the alert, get and write text, dismiss the alert window etc.

187: Is it possible to execute the several instances of WebDriver implementations safely?

Answer:

We can execute multiple instances of web driver though it is not thread-safe. If multiple commands have to be executed, the driver interface has to be accessed after synchronizing the commands. Multiple threading is far better than looping in this case. By creating and managing multiple objects, we can invoke the different browser sections.

188: Using WebDriver, is the interaction with the hidden elements possible?

Answer:

Yes. The hidden elements are not actually hidden, but it is just invisible in the UI. It is done with CSS intentionally for specific reasons. To check this for an element present:

a) *Display:none* (by running this, the element present will be hidden)

b) *Display:block* (by running this, the element hidden will be visible)

189: Why I should migrate from Selenium 1.0 (Selenium RC) to Selenium 2.0 (WebDriver)?

Answer:

Selenium 2.0(WebDriver) is supported by the browser vendors such as Opera, Chrome, Firefox, etc; it imitates user-behaviour closely in comparison to Selenium-1.0 and WebDriver has compact object-oriented APIs. That's reason enough to migrate from Selenium ver 1.0 to Selenium ver 2.0.

190: How come the CSS and XPath locators that worked with Selenium-1.0 do work on Selenium-2.0?

Answer:

The use of native browser procedures could be the reason for complicated XPath locators to be broken. With Selenium-1.0, the Sizzle Library is used to implement the CSS selectors. In Selenium-2.0, the complete capabilities of these are not available. Hence, the CSS and XPath locators that worked with Seleniumver1.0 do work on Seleniumver2.0.

191: Explain how to execute JavaScript in Selenium 2.0.

Answer:

By using the *"JavaScriptExecutor"* you can execute JavaScript in

Selenium-2.0.

For example, to find an element's tag name in Selenium-2.0, you can *execute the following script -*

WebElementmyElement = MyDriver.findElement(By.id("elementLocator"));

String MyStrName = (String) ((JavascriptExecutor) mydriver).executeScript("return arguments[0].tagName", myElement);

192: When I run JavaScript, why does it not return a value?

Answer:

This possibly would happen when you miss out including the *"return"* keyword in your script. The *return* keyword is used while executing your JavaScript.

((JavascriptExecutor) myDriver).executeScript("return window.title;")

193: Are there any operating system restrictions when using the WebDriver?

Answer:

Internet Explorer Driver is used only with Windows while the HTMLUnitDriver, Firefox Driver and the Chrome Driver are usable with any operating system.

194: Explain the architecture of Selenium Webdriver.

Answer:

Selenium Webdriver architecture can be classified into four components. The primary ones are as below -

a) Selenium Client Library where Selenium tools support many languages such as Java, Python and Ruby. Similarly, language binding is used to support many languages.

b) JSON WIRE PROTOCOL over HTTP client where JSON is JavaScript object notation which is used to transfer data particularly with server and client.

c) The Browser Driver which is unique for every browser. It helps to communicate with the browser without showing the logic behind this function. The command sent on the browser driver is executed on the result is given in HTTP form.

d) Browsers supported are Firefox, Internet Explorer and Google Chrome.

195: Explain a *"Remote webdriver server"*.

Answer:

The remote webdriver is an interface where the developer can use or execute the scripts remotely. This is achieved using a *"remote webdriver server"*. There are two parts of remote webdriver - one is server and the other is client. The server is the part which checks for the requests sent by the remote webdriver client. On receiving the requests, it forwards it to the respective browser mentioned in the request. In a local test case, the client libraries contact the browser driver directly and now in remote setting the only difference is that it connects through webdriver server.

196: How to launch remote webdriver server using *my* code?

Answer:

The remote webdriver is started on connection. The URL is pointed to the server running the tests. Below is an example of starting a remote webdriver object pointing to remote webdriver server:

```
require 'selenium-webdriver'
mydriver = Selenium::WebDriver.for :remote, :url => "URL example",
mydriver.get "www.google.com"
mydriver.close
```

197: How is remote webdriver more advantageous than webdriver?

Answer:

A remote webdriver is more advantageous than a webdriver. Since the execution is performed remotely, it can be done on multiple machines at the same time. The tests can be divided based on browsers and then can be run on multiple machines. This helps in parallel testing and takes less time. Another advantage is a better coverage over the code as the distribution would cover almost the entire code.

198: Give an example to show how webdriver is being used.

Answer:

The following example shows the use of webdriver in Java code.

```
public void startApp() throws Exception {
  DesiredCapabilitiesmyCapabilities = new DesiredCapabilities();
  Map<String, Object>myBaseState = new HashMap<>();
  myBaseState.put("type", "NATIVE");
  myBaseState.put("executable", APP);
  myBaseState.put("locator", "//place");
  myCapabilities.setCapability("appdriver-basestate", myBaseState);
  Map<String, Object>myOptions = new HashMap<>();
  myOptions.put("closeOnQuit", true);
```

```
myCapabilities.setCapability("appdriver-options", myOptions);
myDriver = new RemoteWebDriver(new URL("http://localhost:8080"),
myCapabilities);
```

199: Explain the different parts of the Remote WebDriver.

Answer:

The two diverse modes of Remote WebDriver are client and server. In the client mode, the remote instance is connected with the language bindings by using drivers like OperaDriver, FirefoxDriver, and the client of Remote WebDriver functions. In server mode, for setting up the server, the responsibility goes to the language bindings. To this server, the current browser will be connected. The Chrome Driver will be working in this method.

200: Which are the Design Patterns compatible with Selenium-2.0?

Answer:

Page Object Model and the in-build Page Factory Pattern are the two design patterns which are used commonly. With the help of Page Object Model, to interact with each page while test is running, separate classes can be created. Hence these pages can be used again several times whenever there is a need to interact with the pages. Thus, code reusability is one of the main advantages. We need not copy the code while we use the created page specific class. Necessary changes only should be done in one class instead of a whole change in every class, while there is a change in the pages. Thus, maintainability is considered as another merit. In the page object, we are able to use descriptive names which help the code much more readable. By the help of Selenium integrated with Page Factory, we could create the page objects. According to our need, we could make the objects shorter and thus improve the performance.

201: Is there any need to follow the Design patterns for coding the test scripts?

Answer:

With the right design patterns, the experience of coding and running the test scripts will get better. The advantages like code reusability, maintenance, and the readability can be made use of while executing the test or while working. Hence, it is better to follow the design patterns.

202: How can we enable JavaScript when working with HTMLUnitDriver?

Answer:

By default, in the HTMLUnitDriver, JavaScript is not enabled. Hence when we try to execute the JavaScript in the HtmlUNitDriver it will throw an exceptional message or error message and after execution, test result will be *failed*. The error message that will appear when JavaScript is not enabled will be:

'Java.lang.UnsupportedOperationExeception'.

This error can be solved by two ways. During the initialization, we could pass the *true* keyword to the HtmlUnitDriver.

HtmlUNitDrivermyDriver = new HtmlUnitDriver(true);

Else we can use:

HtmlUNitDrivermyDriver = new HtmlUnitDriver();
myDriver.setJavascriptEnabled(true);

203: How can we emulate browser with the HTMLUnitDriver?

Answer:

We can use the HtmlUnitDriver, which is a part of HtmlUnit as the tool for headless browser drivers. Headless browser drivers are similar to other browser drivers but it does not have the graphical user interface (GUI). And so, the execution is not visible. It is very light weight and quick and hence it is used commonly. We are able to emulate a specific browser by using the below given code:

HtmlUnitDrivermyUnitDriver= new HtmlUnitDriver(BrowserVersion.CHROME)

Or

HtmlUnitDrivermyUnitDriver= new HtmlUnitDriver(BrowserVersion.CHROME)

204: Explain how to use the iPhone Driver.

Answer:

By default, we can use the iOS-drivers with the help of simulators. By using these, tests can be run really fast and with flexibility. With Selenium WebDriver, the iOS-drivers are very compatible. Hence, iOS automation is much easier. With Selenium Grid, iOS-drivers are integrated so that the infrastructure of web automation, which is existing, can be reused including helper classes and the utility classes.

205: How to convert Selenium IDE tests scripts to the WebDriver test scripts?

Answer:

At first, we have to record the tests in HTML format with the help of Selenium IDE. Then click on File- Select Export Test Case As- Select the option Java/JUnit/Webdriver. Then File > Save. The file will be saved in .java format. Click and open the file in .java and a java-coded page will be opened.

206: In WebDriver, how can we handle the Untrusted SSL Certificates?

Answer:

Important and sensitive information is passed through the internet in encrypted format so that only the sender and the receiver understand the information. This is done by the SSL certificate. Without using the SSL certificate, the encrypted data can be visible to the system in between the sender and receiver system which is highly critical for the sensitive information or data. By using SSL certificate, we could visit the trustworthy sites without any problems while browsing. For handling the untrusted SSL certificates first, we have to create a FirefoxProfile. In Selenium, *setAcceptUntrustedCertificates()* is a predefined method. So, next we have to make the value of this method as a Boolean true. Then we will be able to open the browser with the help of the Firefoxprofile that we created. Thus, the untrusted certificate can be handled.

207: Using Webdriver, how can we do multiple operations at a time?

Answer:

In Selenium WebDriver, we can work in multiple tabs at once. We can do this by storing the previously handled window in a single variable and then use new tab or window and store the details in another variable. Thus, by using *switchTo* method we can use the multiple tabs or windows. For parallel execution, we can use the features that are provided by TestNG. Tests can be done simultaneously by setting the attribute parallel to the tests in the .xml file. By doing this and clicking on run we can see the tests are running parallel.

208: Explain how to simulate keyboard keys with the help of WebDriver.

Answer:

With the help of the command send_keys, we can stimulate the Keyboard keys in Webdriver. Generally, this is done by Selenium Action Builder. We can stimulate any key to a specific element. The key press should be represented as a symbol while sending the keys. We can avail a list of key symbols.

209: How does Mouse Interaction work in Selenium Webdriver?

Answer:

Mouse events can be handled by Selenium using the ability which is built-in. For doing action events we can use the class org.openqa.selenium.interactions Actions. Thus, there is no need to use keyboard and mouse directly instead we can use the Selenium actions class. The drag and drop, then clicking multiple elements etc are some of the actions included in the API. By using the command *Action action=new Actions(driver);* we can create object *action* in Selenium class. To click on an element the method *click()* is used.

210: Explain the working of Android WebDriver.

Answer:

In Selenium, we get iOS drivers or Appium to work with android. The server of Appium reads the commands from the Java code and these are executed in a real device and on an emulator. There are certain configurations to be done and some jar files to be imported before working with this. In eclipse, create a new Java project and then add jar files to it. Then add the path of the Android APK file to code. With Android Driver, create a WebDriver instance to connect.

Then perform the required actions after finding the elements. After that, quit from the driver. To execute the test, first launch Appium server. Execute the Java program. It will run on the real device or on the emulator.

211: Mention the benefits of using Android WebDriver.

Answer:

There are a number of advantages for Android Webdriver. Take the example of Appium, which is a free and open source tool. It can be downloaded easily. Automation can be done in the mobile applications like native, hybrid and web. The test execution is done on real devices, stimulators and emulators. It can be used cross-platform. It supports a large number of programming languages. There is the availability of record and the playback. Compatible with all testing frameworks.

212: What is Page Object Model or POM?

Answer:

A webpage in Selenium must have a corresponding page class which is responsible to manipulate the elements on the page. POM specifies how to create an object model for the web page. This offers better readability of code, can be used to create multiple instances of testcase, and makes the code available for reuse.

213: Explain Grid2.

Answer:

Selenium grid is a part of Selenium suite which supports testing to be done in different browsers, machines and in different operating system in parallel way, which helps to save the time. Two versions of

Selenium grid are Grid1 and Grid2, where the later one is newer than the other. The Selenium Grid uses the concept of hub-node where the test is run on a machine but the execution is done on diverse machines which are called nodes. Grid2 is bundled with the jar file of Selenium server. There is no necessity of installing Apache Ant in the Grid2. Grid2 can support both the scripts of WebDriver and RC and it is able to automate around five browsers.

214: Explain Page Factory.

Answer:

Page Factory lets you optimize the implementation of the POM. It optimizes the memory utilization of POM. The Page Factory initializes the POM elements using the *initElements* command. Instead of *findelements,* the *findbyelement* is used to find an element.

215: Explain how tests can be run on Grid2.

Answer:

To execute your tests on Grid2, the *RemoteWebDriver* object and the *DesiredCapabilities* object can be used to specify the browser, its version and the platform for testing.

Create intended browser capabilities as:

DesiredCapabilities mycapability = DesiredCapabilities.<browser_name>();

Next step is to pass on the browser properties to the *RemoteWebDriver* object;

WebDriver mydriver = new RemoteWebdriver(new(<hub_path>), mycapability);

After this, the hub shall assign tests to the slave machine.

216: Explain the parameters that are passed on to Grid2.

Answer:

The parameters that can be passed on to Grid2 include:

a) the port specification
b) the timeout specific for the node. Default timeout is 30 seconds after which the hub releases the node if there are no requests.
c) the number of parallel browsers (by default 5) that is allowed to run on a node.

Chapter 6

Selenium Tool Implementation

217: How can you run a test driven by data using Selenium?

Answer:

Selenium does not directly support testing driven by data. But this can be accomplished if the programming language supports. You can use java's jxl library for reading and writing data from an excel file. Another option for testing based on data is to use TestNG's capability.

218: What are the equivalent comparable to a test step, scenario and suite in Selenium?

Answer:

When you use the client driver for Java for Selenium, you can consider the TestNG methods instead of test step. The test tag is the same as the test scenario while the suite tag will be same as the test suite.

219: How are the element attribute value in Selenium obtained?

Answer:

The getAttribute method can be used with Selenium ver 1.0 to get an element's attribute you can use the getAttribute method and specify the element name and maximum length as the parameters.

When it comes to Selenium ver 2.0 you need to use the webdriver's findElement method along with the element's name and its maximum length. Using the css Selector method, you can extract the specific input element's attribute as a string.

220: How are database testing accomplished in Selenium?

Answer:

Though database testing is not supported by Selenium, the programming language binding to Selenium does provide the much-needed support. For example, the JDBC lets you connect to a database, extract and input data to it and also to compare data with the front-end with the Java client.

221: On test execution completion, how can I email the test report?

Answer:

With the ANT tool to build, the 'mail' task can be used to send test results. Hudson which is a Continuous Build Integration tool also allows similar capabilities.

222: How can you make your test scripts more comprehensible?

Answer:

Selenium tests written with hard-coded information make it hard to understand the elements involved in the process execution. In place of typing in the element locators in your tests, you can externalize them. While using Java, the properties file contains the element locators. The locator reference can be specified in the test script, thus making it far more readable.

223: What is the use of a Page Object?

Answer:

Page object essentially distinguishes between the code executing the operations on a page and the code executing the test assertions and verifications. The page object implementation abstracts the page function within a class which defines it. This class definition is extracted during execution to perform page actions. So, when the application layout happens to change, only the navigation part of the test has to be modified while the test function remains intact. This warrants the use of page objects.

This page is intentionally left blank

Chapter **7**

Miscellaneous

224: Mention the benefits of Selenium Git Hub.

Answer:

Here are some of the benefits of Git Hub:

a) Various individuals working together on a single project can post the project data and communicate the same to all team members instantaneously.
b) Jenkins can aid in remotely finishing the project. Thus, you can monitor the failed builds.

225: Explain Desired Capability and how useful is it for Selenium.

Answer:

Desired Capability is a collection of key-value pairs that store the browser's properties like its name, version, system path etc. These are used to check the browser's runtime behaviour. You can use it to configure the Selenium Webdriver instance while the testcases are tried on different browsers, operating systems and versions.

This page is intentionally left blank

HR Interview Questions

Review these typical interview questions and think about how you would answer them. Read the answers listed; you will find best possible answers along with strategies and suggestions

1: Where do you find ideas?

Answer:

Ideas can come from all places, and an interviewer wants to see that your ideas are just as varied. Mention multiple places that you gain ideas from, or settings in which you find yourself brainstorming. Additionally, elaborate on how you record ideas or expand upon them later.

2: How do you achieve creativity in the workplace?

Answer:

It's important to show the interviewer that you're capable of being resourceful and innovative in the workplace, without stepping outside the lines of company values. Explain where ideas normally stem from for you (examples may include an exercise such as list-making or a mind map), and connect this to a particular task in your job that it would be helpful to be creative in.

3: How do you push others to create ideas?

Answer:

If you're in a supervisory position, this may be requiring employees to submit a particular number of ideas, or to complete regular idea-generating exercises, in order to work their creative muscles. However, you can also push others around you to create ideas simply by creating more of your own. Additionally, discuss with the interviewer the importance of questioning people as a way to inspire ideas and change.

4: Describe your creativity.

Answer:

Try to keep this answer within the professional realm, but if you have an impressive background in something creative outside of your employment history, don't be afraid to include it in your answer also. The best answers about creativity will relate problem-solving skills, goal-setting, and finding innovative ways to tackle a project or make a sale in the workplace. However, passions outside of the office are great, too (so long as they don't cut into your work time or mental space).

5: Would you rather receive more authority or more responsibility at work?

Answer:

There are pros and cons to each of these options, and your interviewer will be more interested to see that you can provide a critical answer to the question. Receiving more authority may mean greater decision-making power and may be great for those with outstanding leadership skills, while greater responsibility may be a growth opportunity for those looking to advance steadily throughout their careers.

6: What do you do when someone in a group isn't contributing their fair share?

Answer:

This is a particularly important question if you're interviewing for a position in a supervisory role – explain the ways in which you would identify the problem, and how you would go about pulling aside the individual to discuss their contributions. It's important to understand the process of creating a dialogue, so that you can communicate your expectations clearly to the individual, give them a chance to respond, and to make clear what needs to change. After this, create an action plan with the group member to ensure their contributions are on par with others in the group.

7: Tell me about a time when you made a decision that was outside of your authority.

Answer:

While an answer to this question may portray you as being decisive and confident, it could also identify you to an employer as a potential problem employee. Instead, it may be best to slightly refocus the question into an example of a time that you took on additional responsibilities, and thus had to make decisions that were outside of your normal authority (but which had been granted to you in the specific instance). Discuss how the weight of the decision affected your decision-making process, and the outcomes of the situation.

8: Are you comfortable going to supervisors with disputes?

Answer:

If a problem arises, employers want to know that you will handle it in a timely and appropriate manner. Emphasize that you've rarely had disputes with supervisors in the past, but if a situation were to arise, you feel perfectly comfortable in discussing it with the person in question in order to find a resolution that is satisfactory to both parties.

9: If you had been in charge at your last job, what would you have done differently?

Answer:

No matter how many ideas you have about how things could run better, or opinions on the management at your previous job, remain positive when answering this question. It's okay to show thoughtful reflection on how something could be handled in order to increase efficiency or improve sales, but be sure to keep all of your suggestions focused on making things better, rather than talking about ways to eliminate waste or negativity.

10: Do you believe employers should praise or reward employees for a job well done?

Answer:

Recognition is always great after completing a difficult job, but there are many employers who may ask this question as a way to infer as to whether or not you'll be a high-maintenance worker. While you may appreciate rewards or praise, it's important to convey to the interviewer that you don't require accolades to be confident that you've done your job well. If you are interviewing for a supervisory position where you would be the one praising other employees, highlight the importance of praise in boosting team morale.

11: What do you believe is the most important quality a leader can have?

Answer:

There are many important skills for a leader to have in any business, and the most important component of this question is that you explain why the quality you choose to highlight is important. Try to choose a quality such as communication skills, or an ability to inspire people, and relate it to a specific instance in which you displayed the quality among a team of people.

12: Tell me about a time when an unforeseen problem arose. How did you handle it?

Answer:

It's important that you are resourceful, and level-headed under pressure. An interviewer wants to see that you handle problems systematically, and that you can deal with change in an orderly process. Outline the situation clearly, including all solutions and results of the process you implemented.

13: Can you give me an example of a time when you were able to improve *X objective* at your previous job?

Answer:

It's important here to focus on an improvement you made that created tangible results for your company. Increasing efficiency is certainly a very important element in business, but employers are also looking for concrete results such as increased sales or cut expenses. Explain your process thoroughly, offering specific numbers and evidence wherever possible, particularly in outlining the results.

14: Tell me about a time when a supervisor did not provide specific enough direction on a project.

Answer:

While many employers want their employees to follow very specific guidelines without much decision-making power, it's important also to be able to pick up a project with vague direction and to perform self-sufficiently. Give examples of necessary questions that you asked, and specify how you determined whether a question was something you needed to ask of a supervisor or whether it was something you could determine on your own.

15: Tell me about a time when you were in charge of leading a project.

Answer:

Lead the interviewer through the process of the project, just as you would have with any of your team members. Explain the goal of the project, the necessary steps, and how you delegated tasks to your team. Include the results, and what you learned as a result of the leadership opportunity.

16: Tell me about a suggestion you made to a former employer that was later implemented.

Answer:

Employers want to see that you're interested in improving your company and doing your part – offer a specific example of something you did to create a positive change in your previous job. Explain how you thought of the idea, how your supervisors received it, and what other employees thought was the idea was put into place.

17: Tell me about a time when you thought of a way something in the workplace could be done more efficiently.

Answer:

Focus on the positive aspects of your idea. It's important not to portray your old company or boss negatively, so don't elaborate on how inefficient a particular system was. Rather, explain a situation in which you saw an opportunity to increase productivity or to streamline a process, and explain in a general step-by-step how you implemented a better system.

18: Is there a difference between leading and managing people – which is your greater strength?

Answer:

There is a difference – leaders are often great idea people, passionate, charismatic, and with the ability to organize and inspire others, while managers are those who ensure a system runs, facilitate its operations, make authoritative decisions, and who take great responsibility for all aspects from overall success to the finest decisions. Consider which of these is most applicable to the position, and explain how you fit into this role, offering concrete examples of your past experience.

19: Do you function better in a leadership role, or as a worker on a team?

Answer:

It is important to consider what qualities the interviewer is looking for in your position, and to express how you embody this role. If you're a leader, highlight your great ideas, drive and passion, and ability to incite others around you to action. If you work great in teams, focus on your dedication to the task at hand, your cooperation and communication skills, and your ability to keep things

20: Tell me about a time when you discovered something in the workplace that was disrupting your (or others) productivity – what did you do about it?

Answer:

Try to not focus on negative aspects of your previous job too much, but instead choose an instance in which you found a positive, and quick, solution to increase productivity. Focus on the way you noticed the opportunity, how you presented a solution to your supervisor, and then how the change was implemented (most importantly, talk about how you led the change initiative). This is a great opportunity for you to display your problem-solving skills, as well as your resourceful nature and leadership skills.

21: How do you perform in a job with clearly-defined objectives and goals?

Answer:

It is important to consider the position when answering this question clearly, it is best if you can excel in a job with clearly-defined objectives and goals (particularly if you're in an entry level or sales position). However, if you're applying for a position with a leadership role or creative aspect to it, be sure to focus on the ways that you additionally enjoy the challenges of developing and implementing your own ideas.

22: How do you perform in a job where you have great decision-making power?

Answer:

The interviewer wants to know that, if hired, you won't be the type of employee who needs constant supervision or who asks for advice, authority, or feedback every step of the way. Explain that you work well in a decisive, productive environment, and that you look forward to taking initiative in your position.

23: If you saw another employee doing something dishonest or unethical, what would you do?

Answer:

In the case of witnessing another employee doing something dishonest, it is always best to act in accordance with company policies for such a situation – and if you don't know what this company's specific policies are, feel free to simply state that you would handle it according to the policy and by reporting it to the appropriate persons in charge. If you are aware of the company's policies (such as if you are seeking a promotion within your own company), it is best to specifically outline your actions according to the policy.

24: Tell me about a time when you learned something on your own that later helped in your professional life.

Answer:

This question is important because it allows the interviewer to gain insight into your dedication to learning and advancement. Choose an example solely from your personal life, and provide a brief anecdote ending in the lesson you learned. Then, explain in a clear and thorough manner how this lesson has translated into a usable skill or practice in your position.

25: Tell me about a time when you developed a project idea at work.

Answer:

Choose a project idea that you developed that was typical of projects you might complete in the new position. Outline where your idea came from, the type of research you did to ensure its success and relevancy, steps that were included in the project, and the end results. Offer specific before and after statistics, to show its success.

26: Tell me about a time when you took a risk on a project.

Answer:

Whether the risk involved something as complex as taking on a major project with limited resources or time, or simply volunteering for a task that was outside your field of experience, show that you are willing to stretch out of your comfort zone and to try new things. Offer specific examples of why something you did was risky, and explain what you learned in the process – or how this prepared you for a job objective you later faced in your career.

27: What would you tell someone who was looking to get into this field?

Answer:

This question allows you to be the expert – and will show the interviewer that you have the knowledge and experience to go along with any training and education on your resume. Offer your knowledge as advice of unexpected things that someone entering the field may encounter, and be sure to end with positive advice such as the passion or dedication to the work that is required to truly succeed.

28: Tell me about a time when you worked additional hours to finish a project.

Answer:

It's important for your employer to see that you are dedicated to your work, and willing to put in extra hours when required or when a job calls for it. However, be careful when explaining why you were called to work additional hours – for instance, did you have to stay late because you set goals poorly earlier in the process? Or on a more positive note, were you working additional hours because a client requested for a deadline to be moved up on short notice? Stress your competence and willingness to give 110% every time.

29: Tell me about a time when your performance exceeded the duties and requirements of your job.

Answer:

If you're a great candidate for the position, this should be an easy question to answer – choose a time when you truly went above and beyond the call of duty, and put in additional work or voluntarily took on new responsibilities. Remain humble, and express gratitude for the learning opportunity, as well as confidence in your ability to give a repeat performance.

30: What is your driving attitude about work?

Answer:

There are many possible good answers to this question, and the interviewer primarily wants to see that you have a great passion for the job and that you will remain motivated in your career if hired. Some specific driving forces behind your success may include hard work, opportunity, growth potential, or success.

31: Do you take work home with you?

Answer:

It is important to first clarify that you are always willing to take work home when necessary, but you want to emphasize as well that it has not been an issue for you in the past. Highlight skills such as time management, goal-setting, and multi-tasking, which can all ensure that work is completed at work.

32: Describe a typical work day to me.

Answer:

There are several important components in your typical work day, and an interviewer may derive meaning from any or all of them, as well as from your ability to systematically lead him or her through the day. Start at the beginning of your day and proceed chronologically, making sure to emphasize steady productivity, time for review, goal-setting, and prioritizing, as well as some additional time to account for unexpected things that may arise.

33: Tell me about a time when you went out of your way at your previous job.

Answer:

Here it is best to use a specific example of the situation that required you to go out of your way, what your specific position would have required that you did, and how you went above that. Use concrete details, and be sure to include the results, as well as reflection on what you learned in the process.

34: Are you open to receiving feedback and criticisms on your job performance, and adjusting as necessary?

Answer:

This question has a pretty clear answer – yes – but you'll need to display a knowledge as to why this is important. Receiving feedback and criticism is one thing, but the most important part of that process is to then implement it into your daily work. Keep a good attitude, and express that you always appreciate constructive feedback.

35: What inspires you?

Answer:

You may find inspiration in nature, reading success stories, or mastering a difficult task, but it's important that your inspiration is positively-based and that you're able to listen and tune into it when it appears. Keep this answer generally based in the professional world, but where applicable, it may stretch a bit into creative exercises in your personal life that, in turn, help you in achieving career objectives.

36: How do you inspire others?

Answer:

This may be a difficult question, as it is often hard to discern the effects of inspiration in others. Instead of offering a specific example of a time when you inspired someone, focus on general principles such as leading by example that you employ in your professional life. If possible, relate this to a quality that someone who inspired you possessed, and discuss the way you have modified or modeled it in your own work.

37: How do you make decisions?

Answer:

This is a great opportunity for you to wow your interviewer with your decisiveness, confidence, and organizational skills. Make sure that you outline a process for decision-making, and that you stress the importance of weighing your options, as well as in trusting intuition. If you answer this question skilfully and with ease, your interviewer will trust in your capability as a worker.

38: What are the most difficult decisions for you to make?

Answer:

Explain your relationship to decision-making, and a general synopsis of the process you take in making choices. If there is a particular type of decision that you often struggle with, such as those that involve other people, make sure to explain why that type of decision is tough for you, and how you are currently engaged in improving your skills.

39: When making a tough decision, how do you gather information?

Answer:

If you're making a tough choice, it's best to gather information from as many sources as possible. Lead the interviewer through your process of taking information from people in different areas, starting first with advice from experts in your field, feedback from co-workers or other clients, and by looking analytically at your own past experiences.

40: Tell me about a decision you made that did not turn out well.

Answer:

Honesty and transparency are great values that your interviewer will appreciate – outline the choice you made, why you made it, the results of your poor decision – and finally (and most importantly!) what you learned from the decision. Give the interviewer reason to trust that you wouldn't make a decision like that again in the future.

41: Are you able to make decisions quickly?

Answer:

You may be able to make decisions quickly, but be sure to communicate your skill in making sound, thorough decisions as well. Discuss the importance of making a decision quickly, and how you do so, as well as the necessity for each decision to first be well-informed.

42: Ten years ago, what were your career goals?

Answer:

In reflecting back to what your career goals were ten years ago, it's important to show the ways in which you've made progress in that time. Draw distinct links between specific objectives that you've achieved, and speak candidly about how it felt to reach those goals. Remain positive, upbeat, and growth-oriented, even if you haven't yet achieved all of the goals you set out to reach.

43: Tell me about a weakness you used to have, and how you changed it.

Answer:

Choose a non-professional weakness that you used to have, and outline the process you went through in order to grow past it. Explain the weakness itself, why it was problematic, the action steps you planned, how you achieved them, and the end result.

44: Tell me about your goal-setting process.

Answer:

When describing your goal-setting process, clearly outline the way that you create an outline for yourself. It may be helpful to offer an example of a particular goal you've set in the past, and use this as a starting point to guide the way you created action steps, check-in points, and how the goal was eventually achieved.

45: Tell me about a time when you solved a problem by creating actionable steps to follow.

Answer:

This question will help the interviewer to see how you talented you are in outlining, problem resolution, and goal-setting. Explain thoroughly the procedure of outlining the problem, establishing steps to take, and then how you followed the steps (such as through check-in points along the way, or intermediary goals).

46: Where do you see yourself five years from now?

Answer:

Have some idea of where you would like to have advanced to in the position you're applying for, over the next several years. Make sure that your future plans line up with you still working for the company, and stay positive about potential advancement. Focus on future opportunities, and what you're looking forward to – but make sure your reasons for advancement are admirable, such as greater experience and the chance to learn, rather than simply being out for a higher salary.

47: When in a position, do you look for opportunities to promote?

Answer:

There's a fine balance in this question – you want to show the interviewer that you have initiative and motivation to advance in your career, but not at the expense of appearing opportunistic or selfishly-motivated. Explain that you are always open to growth opportunities, and very willing to take on new responsibilities as your career advances.

48: On a scale of 1 to 10, how successful has your life been?

Answer:

Though you may still have a long list of goals to achieve, it's important to keep this answer positively-focused. Choose a high number between 7 and 9, and explain that you feel your life has been largely successful and satisfactory as a result of several specific achievements or experiences. Don't go as high as a 10, as the interviewer may not believe your response or in your ability to reason critically.

49: What is your greatest goal in life?

Answer:

It's okay for this answer to stray a bit into your personal life, but best if you can keep it professionally-focused. While specific goals are great, if your personal goal doesn't match up exactly with one of the company's objectives, you're better off keeping your goal a little more generic and encompassing, such as "success in my career" or "leading a happy and fulfilling life." Keep your answer brief, and show a decisive nature – most importantly, make it clear that you've already thought about this question and know what you want.

50: Tell me about a time when you set a goal in your personal life and achieved it.

Answer:

The interviewer can see that you excel at setting goals in your professional life, but he or she also wants to know that you are consistent in your life and capable of setting goals outside of the office as well. Use an example such as making a goal to eat more healthily or to drink more water, and discuss what steps you outlined to achieve your goal, the process of taking action, and the final results as well.

51: What is your greatest goal in your career?

Answer:

Have a very specific goal of something you want to achieve in your career in mind, and be sure that it's something the position clearly puts you in line to accomplish. Offer the goal as well as your plans to get there, and emphasize clear ways in which this position will be an opportunity to work toward the goal.

52: Tell me about a time when you achieved a goal.

Answer:

Start out with how you set the goal, and why you chose it. Then, take the interviewer through the process of outlining the goal, taking steps to achieve it, the outcome, and finally, how you felt after achieving it or recognition you received. The most important part of this question includes the planning and implementation of strategies, so focus most of your time on explaining these aspects. However, the preliminary decisions and end results are also important, so make sure to include them as well.

53: What areas of your work would you still like to improve in? What are your plans to do this?

Answer:

While you may not want the interviewer to focus on things you could improve on, it's important to be self-aware of your own growth opportunities. More importantly, you can impress an interviewer by having specific goals and actions outlined in order to facilitate your growth, even if your area of improvement is something as simple as increasing sales or finding new ways to create greater efficiency.

54: Tell me about your favorite book or newspaper.

Answer:

The interviewer will look at your answer to this question in order to determine your ability to analyze and review critically. Additionally, try to choose something that is on a topic related to your field or that embodies a theme important to your work, and be able to explain how it relates. Stay away from controversial subject matter, such as politics or religion.

55: If you could be rich or famous, which would you choose?

Answer:

This question speaks to your ability to think creatively, but your answer may also give great insight to your character. If you answer rich, your interviewer may interpret that you are self-confident and don't seek approval from others, and that you like to be rewarded for your work. If you choose famous, your interviewer may gather that you like to be well-known and to deal with people, and to have the platform to deliver your message to others. Either way, it's important to back up your answer with sound reasoning.

56: If you could trade places with anyone for a week, who would it be and why?

Answer:

This question is largely designed to test your ability to think on your feet, and to come up with a reasonable answer to an outside the box question. Whoever you choose, explain your answer in a logical manner, and offer specific professional reasons that led you to choose the individual.

57: What would you say if I told you that just from glancing over your resume, I can already see three spelling mistakes?

Answer:

Clearly, your resume should be absolutely spotless – and you should be confident that it is. If your interviewer tries to make you second-guess yourself here, remain calm and poised and assert with a polite smile that you would be quite surprised as you are positive that your resume is error-free.

58: Tell me about your worldview.

Answer:

This question is designed to offer insight into your personality, so be aware of how the interviewer will interpret your answer. Speak openly and directly, and try to incorporate your own job skills into your outlook on life. For example, discuss your beliefs on the ways that hard work and dedication can always bring success, or in how learning new things is one of life's greatest gifts. It's okay to expand into general life principles here, but try to keep your thoughts related to the professional field as well.

59: What is the biggest mistake someone could make in an interview?

Answer:

The biggest mistake that could be made in an interview is to be caught off guard! Make sure that you don't commit whatever you answer here, and additionally be prepared for all questions. Other common mistakes include asking too early in the hiring process about job benefits, not having questions prepared when the interviewer asks if you have questions, arriving late, dressing casually or sloppily, or showing ignorance of the position.

60: If you won the $50m lottery, what would you do with the money?

Answer:

While a question such as this may seem out of place in a job interview, it's important to display your creative thinking and your ability to think on the spot. It's also helpful if you choose something admirable, yet believable, to do with the money such as donate the first seventy percent to a charitable cause, and divide the remainder among gifts for friends, family, and of course, yourself.

61: Is there ever a time when honesty isn't appropriate in the workplace?

Answer:

This may be a difficult question, but the only time that honesty isn't appropriate in the workplace is perhaps when you're feeling anger or another emotion that is best kept to yourself. If this is the case, explain simply that it is best to put some thoughts aside, and clarify that the process of keeping some thoughts quiet is often enough to smooth over any unsettled emotions, thus eliminating the problem.

62: If you could travel anywhere in the world, where would it be?

Answer:

This question is meant to allow you to be creative – so go ahead and stretch your thoughts to come up with a unique answer. However, be sure to keep your answer professionally-minded. For example, choose somewhere rich with culture or that would expose you to a new experience, rather than going on an expensive cruise through the Bahamas.

63: What would I find in your refrigerator right now?

Answer:

An interviewer may ask a creative question such as this in order to discern your ability to answer unexpected questions calmly, or, to try to gain some insight into your personality. For example, candidates with a refrigerator full of junk food or take-out may be more likely to be under stress or have health issues, while a candidate with a balanced refrigerator full of nutritious staples may be more likely to lead a balanced mental life, as well.

64: If you could play any sport professionally, what would it be and what aspect draws you to it?

Answer:

Even if you don't know much about professional sports, this question might be a great opportunity to highlight some of your greatest professional working skills. For example, you may choose to play professional basketball, because you admire the teamwork and coordination that goes into creating a solid play. Or, you may choose to play professional tennis, because you consider yourself to be a go-getter with a solid work ethic and great dedication to perfecting your craft. Explain your choice simply to the interviewer without elaborating on drawn-out sports metaphors, and be sure to point out specific areas or skills in which you excel.

65: Who were the presidential and vice-presidential candidates in the 2008 elections?

Answer:

This question, plain and simple, is intended as a gauge of your intelligence and awareness. If you miss this question, you may well fail the interview. Offer your response with a polite smile, because you understand that there are some individuals who probably miss this question.

66: Explain X task in a few short sentences as you would to a second-grader.

Answer:

An interviewer may ask you to break down a normal job task that you would complete in a manner that a child could understand, in part to test your knowledge of the task's inner workings – but in larger part, to test your ability to explain a process in simple, basic terms. While you and your co-workers may be able to converse using highly technical language, being able to simplify a process is an important skill for any employee to have.

67: If you could compare yourself to any animal, what would it be?

Answer:

Many interviewers ask this question, and it's not to determine which character traits you think you embody – instead, the interviewer wants to see that you can think outside the box, and that you're able to reason your way through any situation. Regardless of what animal you answer, be sure that you provide a thorough reason for your choice.

68: Who is your hero?

Answer:

Your hero may be your mother or father, an old professor– but keep your reasoning for your choice professional, and be prepared to offer a logical train of thought. Choose someone who embodies values that are important in your chosen career field, and answer the question with a smile and sense of passion.

69: Who would play you in the movie about your life?

Answer:

As with many creative questions that challenge an interviewee to think outside the box, the answer to this question is not as important as how you answer it. Choose a professional, and relatively non-controversial actor or actress, and then be prepared to offer specific reasoning for your choice, employing important skills or traits you possess.

70: Name five people, alive or dead, that would be at your ideal dinner party.

Answer:

Smile and sound excited at the opportunity to think outside the box when asked this question, even if it seems to come from left field. Choose dynamic, inspiring individuals who you could truly learn from, and explain what each of them would have to offer to the conversation. Don't forget to include yourself, and to talk about what you would bring to the conversation as well!

71: What is customer service?

Answer:

Customer service can be many things – and the most important consideration in this question is that you have a creative answer. Demonstrate your ability to think outside the box by offering a confident answer that goes past a basic definition, and that shows you have truly considered your own individual view of what it means to take care of your customers. The thoughtful consideration you hold for customers will speak for itself.

72: Tell me about a time when you went out of your way for a customer.

Answer:

It's important that you offer an example of a time you truly went out of your way – be careful not to confuse something that felt like a big effort on your part, with something your employer would expect you to do anyway. Offer an example of the customer's problems, what you did to solve it, and the way the customer responded after you took care of the situation.

73: How do you gain confidence from customers?

Answer:

This is a very open-ended question that allows you to show your customer service skills to the interviewer. There are many possible answers, and it is best to choose something that you've had great experience with, such as "by handling situations with transparency," "offering rewards," or "focusing on great communication." Offer specific examples of successes you've had.

74: Tell me about a time when a customer was upset or agitated – how did you handle the situation?

Answer:

Similar to handling a dispute with another employee, the most important part to answering this question is to first set up the scenario, offer a step-by-step guide to your particular conflict resolution style, and end by describing the way the conflict was resolved. Be sure that in answering questions about your own conflict resolution style, that you emphasize the importance of open communication and understanding from both parties, as well as a willingness to reach a compromise or other solution.

75: When can you make an exception for a customer?

Answer:

Exceptions for customers can generally be made when in accordance with company policy or when directed by a supervisor. Display an understanding of the types of situations in which an exception should be considered, such as when a customer has endured a particular hardship, had a complication with an order, or at a request.

76: What would you do in a situation where you were needed by both a customer and your boss?

Answer:

While both your customer and your boss have different needs of you and are very important to your success as a worker, it is always best to try to attend to your customer first – however, the key is explaining to your boss why you are needed urgently by the customer, and then to assure your boss that you will attend to his or her needs as soon as possible (unless it's absolutely an urgent matter).

77: What is the most important aspect of customer service?

Answer:

While many people would simply state that customer satisfaction is the most important aspect of customer service, it's important to be able to elaborate on other important techniques in customer service situations. Explain why customer service is such a key part of business, and be sure to expand on the aspect that you deem to be the most important in a way that is reasoned and well-thought out.

78: Is it best to create low or high expectations for a customer?

Answer:

You may answer this question either way (after, of course, determining that the company does not have a clear opinion on the matter). However, no matter which way you answer the question, you must display a thorough thought process, and very clear reasoning for the option you chose. Offer pros and cons of each and include the ultimate point that tips the scale in favor of your chosen answer.

INDEX

Selenium Testing Tools Interview Questions

Generic Selenium

Selenium IDE

52: How to print the stored evaluation result in Selenium to confirm its value?

53: Explain how to handle JavaScript alert.

54: How to move my recorded XPath test to Selenium CSS locator?

55: I have scripted an element locator of my own. How to test the same?

56: Can the js extension be plugged into Selenium?

57: Explain the process for converting the tests for Selenium IDE from Selenese to some other language.

58: Why am I unable to execute my converted Selenium IDE Tests in Java? Why am I unable to execute the options? Why is the Table tab of Selenium IDE disabled?

59: How can I use Selenese only as my test script language and also run tests in other browsers?

60: How can we test a new command added in the middle of a program?

61: Can you specify where the Selenium IDE tests should start test execution?

62: What are the tools available (other than Selenium IDE) to test element locators?

63: What are some of Selenium IDE's advanced upcoming features?

64: Explain how loops are used for flow-control in Selenium IDE.

65: Can screen coordinates be used with the click command, to click a particular portion of an element?

66: Explain how the drop-down option presence can be verified in Selenium.

67: In Selenium IDE, how to store information on a HTML table?

68: Is it conceivable to have a high priority CSS-Locator in Selenium-IDE while recording and displaying the CSS and other locators?

69: How can we handle the dynamic alerts that appear on screen?

70: Is right click allowed on a locator?

71: How are screenshots of a page captured by means of Selenium IDE?

72: Can the test execution be delayed after a particular command?

73: Explain page timeout and how it affects the Selenium script.

74: Differentiate – type and type keys.

Selenium RC (Selenium 1.0)

98: Will Selenium RC work on UNIX/Mac?

99: Can we execute the test scripts in newly created experimental browsers? If yes, how?

100: After executing test cases, why don't I see the generated test report?

101: Does Selenium have recovery scenarios similar to QTP?

102: How do I iterate through my test script?

103: How do I count the number of images on my page?

104: What are the existing choices while starting Selenium Server?

105: Can you run your test-code using your own Firefox profile?

106: How is the Selenium server's log captured?

107: Explain Heightened Privilege Browsers.

108: How to manage an application with many popup windows?

109: When you execute a Firefox test, an error shows up that Firefox won't shut down when it is getting a profile ready. How to resolve this error?

110: Using Selenium RC, how can we execute the tests which contain AJAX operations?

111: During the execution of a test, can we upload files, for example, Word file?

112: While running Selenium tests "permission denied error" is displayed. What can be the reason for this?

113: Elements cannot be located using the "style" attribute with Internet Explorer. Why?

114: What are the technical drawbacks of Selenium RC?

115: Can testing code use objects outside the browser if required and how?

116: Can Selenium be used for browsers on mobile devices?

117: What are the advantages of Selenium RC compared to other tools?

118: What are the disadvantages of using Selenium RC?

119: How can we run two tests on diverse browsers on the same operating system with Selenium RC?

Selenium Grid

120: When is the Selenium Grid more advantageous?

121: Can you record the Selenium Grid test cases from other machines? Explain how?

122: Explain the working of Selenium Grid.

123: Which component in Selenium Grid routes the requests in Selenese from the test?

124: How many maximum browsers can parallel-run on a Selenium node?

125: What is the default number for hub port assigned?

126: Can you create test Cases using test design in Selenium Grid?

127: What is the default Selenium Grid timeout?

128: Can Selenium RC and/or Selenium Webdriver test cases be executed in parallel using Selenium Grid?

129: Can Selenium IDE Test cases be executed using Selenium Grid?

130: Explain the two major Selenium Grid elements.

131: How many hubs are available in Selenium Grid?

132: How many nodes are available in Selenium Grid?

133: How to specify the browser and OS information in Selenium Grid?

134: How to reduce the test execution time of Selenium tests, when the test is executed using various machines and browsers?

135: Explain the working of Selenium Grid.

136: Picturize the functionality of Selenium grid.

137: How do you configure Selenium Grid Hub?

138: How do you configure Selenium Grid Node?

139: How can you start the Selenium Grid Slave Server?

140: Can you start the Selenium grid's slave from another port than the typical 5555?

141: How can you start the Selenium grid slaves on different systems so that the hub can be controlled by the local host?

142: Can an environment be specified when you start the grid slave?

143: How do you use Selenium test configuration specific to a machine?

144: How can you map a name like 'Safari on Mac' to Safari Browser?

145: How will the Selenium grid hub contact the RC slave?

146: The RC slave can, at times, become unresponsive while the Selenium grid hub waits for the its response. How does the hub recognise to leave the waiting RC slave afterwards a while?

147: What happens if the hub becomes unavailable when the Selenium RC slaves are running?

148: Can you use the Selenium grid for performance testing?

149: While working with Selenium Grid, can we use additional logs?

150: How can you run the RC Slave in single-window mode?

151: A similar RC slave is displayed multiple times in the hub console. What may be the reasons for these duplicate entries?

152: During the initialization of Selenium grid, is it possible to set the corporate proxy?

153: While using languages such as .Net, Ruby, or Java, how can Selenium drivers be used?

154: What do you know of the test reports while using Selenium grid to execute a test?

Web Driver (Selenium 2.0)

155: Explain the limitations if any while inoculating competences in WebDriver to run tests on browser that is not reinforced by WebDriver.

156: Explain the various exceptions in Selenium WebDriver.

157: Explain the variety of WAIT statements in Selenium WebDriver.

158: Which API is essential for Selenium Webdriver Database Testing?

159: Explain the Selenium WebDriver Listeners.

160: Explain the buzzword Selenium ver 2.0.

161: Why do you need to combine two tools as Selenium ver 2.0?

162: Will everyone be using Selenium ver 2.0?

163: How can you specify Selenium ver 2.0 browser configurations?

164: Differentiate between Selenium ver 2.0 and Selenium ver 1.0 configuration.

165: Give a coding example for starting Selenium ver 2.0 for testing.

166: In Selenium Webdriver, which one has the fastest implementation?

167: What are the different types of element locators present in Selenium ver 2.0?

168: How would you submit a Selenium form?

169: How would you stimulate the keyboard keys by pressing with the help of Selenium ver 2.0?

170: Explain how to clear the content of the textbox with the help of Selenium ver 2.0.

171: Using Selenium ver 2.0, how do you choose a value in drop down list?

172: While working with Selenium ver 2.0 there may be popup windows displayed. Explain the options to deal with it.

173: With the help of Selenium ver 2.0, how to handle frames?

174: Is navigating forward and backward in a Selenium ver 2.0 browser possible?

175: Which is the fastest WebDriver browser implementation order?

176: Can you use Selenium ver 2.0 with Selenium RC API?

177: Explain with an example – using Selenium ver 1 in Selenium 2.

178: Selenium ver 1.0 had many supporting browsers whereas Selenium ver 2.0 only has a few. How do I use a particular browser with Selenium ver 2.0?

179: Are there any restrictions when augmenting the webdriver abilities while performing browser-based tests?

180: Can the user agent be changed in FireFox browser as the tests to be performed need to check the setting of user agent?

181: Do different employments of the webdriver have different XPath implementations?

182: What can be done if the application is using AJAX largely, due to which the tests are getting timed out when Selenium 2.0 is in use?

183: Can anything else be used instead of implicit wait when wait is required for elements?

184: Explain what and when to use RemoteWebDriver.

185: Which languages are supported by WebDriver?

186: Using Selenium WebDriver, explain the method to handle JavaScript alert.

187: Is it possible to execute the several instances of WebDriver implementations safely?

188: Using WebDriver, is the interaction with the hidden elements possible?

189: Why I should migrate from Selenium 1.0 (Selenium RC) to Selenium 2.0 (WebDriver)?

190: How come the CSS and XPath locators that worked with Selenium-1.0 do work on Selenium-2.0?

191: Explain how to execute JavaScript in Selenium-2.0.

192: When I run JavaScript, why does it not return a value?

193: Are there any operating system restrictions when using the WebDriver?
194: Explain the architecture of Selenium Webdriver.
195: Explain a "Remote webdriver server".
196: How to launch remote webdriver server using my code?
197: How is remote webdriver more advantageous than webdriver?
198: Give an example to show how webdriver is being used.
199: Explain the different parts of the Remote WebDriver.
200: Which are the Design Patterns compatible with Selenium-2.0?
201: Is there any need to follow the Design patterns for coding the test scripts?
202: How can we enable JavaScript when working with HTMLUnitDriver?
203: How can we emulate browser with the HTMLUnitDriver?
204: Explain how to use the iPhone Driver.
205: How to convert Selenium IDE tests scripts to the WebDriver test scripts?
206: In WebDriver, how can we handle the Untrusted SSL Certificates?
207: Using Webdriver, how can we do multiple operations at a time?
208: Explain how to simulate keyboard keys with the help of WebDriver.
209: How does Mouse Interaction work in Selenium Webdriver?
210: Explain the working of Android WebDriver.
211: Mention the benefits of using Android WebDriver.
212: What is Page Object Model or POM?
213: Explain Grid2.
214: Explain Page Factory.
215: Explain how tests can be run on Grid2.
216: Explain the parameters that are passed on to Grid2.

Selenium Tool Implementation

217: How can you run a test driven by data using Selenium?
218: What are the equivalent comparable to a test step, scenario and suite in Selenium?
219: How are the element attribute value in Selenium obtained?
220: How are database testing accomplished in Selenium?

Miscellaneous

HR Interview Questions

1: Where do you find ideas?

2: How do you achieve creativity in the workplace?

3: How do you push others to create ideas?

4: Describe your creativity.

5: Would you rather receive more authority or more responsibility at work?

6: What do you do when someone in a group isn't contributing their fair share?

7: Tell me about a time when you made a decision that was outside of your authority.

8: Are you comfortable going to supervisors with disputes?

9: If you had been in charge at your last job, what would you have done differently?

10: Do you believe employers should praise or reward employees for a job well done?

11: What do you believe is the most important quality a leader can have?

12: Tell me about a time when an unforeseen problem arose. How did you handle it?

13: Can you give me an example of a time when you were able to improve X objective at your previous job?

14: Tell me about a time when a supervisor did not provide specific enough direction on a project.

15: Tell me about a time when you were in charge of leading a project.

16: Tell me about a suggestion you made to a former employer that was later implemented.

17: Tell me about a time when you thought of a way something in the workplace could be done more efficiently.

18: Is there a difference between leading and managing people – which is your greater strength?

19: Do you function better in a leadership role, or as a worker on a team?

20: Tell me about a time when you discovered something in the workplace that was disrupting your (or others) productivity – what did you do about it?

47: When in a position, do you look for opportunities to promote?

48: On a scale of 1 to 10, how successful has your life been?

49: What is your greatest goal in life?

50: Tell me about a time when you set a goal in your personal life and achieved it.

51: What is your greatest goal in your career?

52: Tell me about a time when you achieved a goal.

53: What areas of your work would you still like to improve in? What are your plans to do this?

54: Tell me about your favorite book or newspaper.

55: If you could be rich or famous, which would you choose?

56: If you could trade places with anyone for a week, who would it be and why?

57: What would you say if I told you that just from glancing over your resume, I can already see three spelling mistakes?

58: Tell me about your worldview.

59: What is the biggest mistake someone could make in an interview?

60: If you won the $50m lottery, what would you do with the money?

61: Is there ever a time when honesty isn't appropriate in the workplace?

62: If you could travel anywhere in the world, where would it be?

63: What would I find in your refrigerator right now?

64: If you could play any sport professionally, what would it be and what aspect draws you to it?

65: Who were the presidential and vice-presidential candidates in the 2008 elections?

66: Explain X task in a few short sentences as you would to a second-grader.

67: If you could compare yourself to any animal, what would it be?

68: Who is your hero?

69: Who would play you in the movie about your life?

70: Name five people, alive or dead, that would be at your ideal dinner party.

71: What is customer service?

72: Tell me about a time when you went out of your way for a customer.

Some of the following titles might also be handy:

48. Mac OS X Snow Leopard Interview Questions You'll Most Likely Be Asked
49. Microsoft Access Interview Questions You'll Most Likely Be Asked
50. Microsoft PowerPoint Interview Questions You'll Most Likely Be Asked
51. Microsoft Word Interview Questions You'll Most Likely Be Asked
52. MySQL Interview Questions You'll Most Likely Be Asked
53. Networking Interview Questions You'll Most Likely Be Asked
54. OOPS Interview Questions You'll Most Likely Be Asked
55. Operating Systems Interview Questions You'll Most Likely Be Asked
56. Oracle Database Administration Interview Questions You'll Most Likely Be Asked
57. Oracle E-Business Suite Interview Questions You'll Most Likely Be Asked
58. ORACLE PL/SQL Interview Questions You'll Most Likely Be Asked
59. Perl Programming Interview Questions You'll Most Likely Be Asked
60. PHP Interview Questions You'll Most Likely Be Asked
61. Python Interview Questions You'll Most Likely Be Asked
62. RESTful JAVA Web Services Interview Questions You'll Most Likely Be Asked
63. SAP HANA Interview Questions You'll Most Likely Be Asked
64. SAS Interview Questions You'll Most Likely Be Asked
65. SAS Programming Guidelines Interview Questions You'll Most Likely Be Asked
66. Selenium Testing Tools Interview Questions You'll Most Likely Be Asked
67. Silverlight Interview Questions You'll Most Likely Be Asked
68. Software Repositories Interview Questions You'll Most Likely Be Asked
69. Software Testing Interview Questions You'll Most Likely Be Asked
70. SQL Server Interview Questions You'll Most Likely Be Asked
71. Tomcat Interview Questions You'll Most Likely Be Asked
72. UML Interview Questions You'll Most Likely Be Asked
73. Unix Interview Questions You'll Most Likely Be Asked
74. UNIX Shell Programming Interview Questions You'll Most Likely Be Asked
75. Windows Server 2008 R2 Interview Questions You'll Most Likely Be Asked
76. XLXP, XSLT, XPATH, XFORMS & XQuery Interview Questions You'll Most Likely Be Asked
77. XML Interview Questions You'll Most Likely Be Asked

NOTES

45641795R00085

Printed in Poland
by Amazon Fulfillment
Poland Sp. z o.o., Wrocław